"A well-told, powerful story." –R. Crumb

"Stunning. Horrifying. Beautifully done." –Alison Bechdel

"A solid job. Putrid serial killer Jeffrey Dahmer's origins are explored in this
fine book. Dig it—it'll hang you out to dry."
–James Ellroy

"This one's still haunting me." –Brad Meltzer

"A brilliant graphic novel and surely ranks among the very best of the form."
–Dan Chaon

"It wasn't easy reading this book, but I'm glad I did."
–David Small

"*My Friend Dahmer* will certainly quench your dark little desires."
–Chuck Klosterman

"Wow. Reading this is unlike any other reading experience I've ever had. Do it."
–Rainn Wilson

★ "A small, dark classic." –*Publishers Weekly* (starred review)

★ "An exemplary demonstration of the transformative possibilities of
graphic narrative."
–*Kirkus* (starred review)

"One of the most thought-provoking comics released in a long time."
–Slate.com

"Astounding." –Lev Grossman, *TIME*

"One of the best graphic novels I've read this year." –*USA Today*

"Masterful . . . a rich tale full of complexity and sensitivity."
–*The Cleveland Plain Dealer*

ALSO BY DERF BACKDERF

My Friend Dahmer

TRASHED

a graphic novel by
DERF BACKDERF

Abrams ComicArts, New York

EDITOR: Charles Kochman
DESIGNER: Pamela Notarantonio
MANAGING EDITOR: Jen Graham
PRODUCTION MANAGER: Kathy Lovisolo

Library of Congress Cataloging-in-Publication Data
Backderf, Derf.
  Trashed : a graphic novel / by Derf Backderf.
    pages cm
  Summary: Graphic novel based on the author's time spent working on a garbage truck.
  ISBN 978-1-4197-1453-5 (hardcover) — ISBN 978-1-4197-1454-2 (pbk.) —
  ISBN 978-1-61312-865-7 (ebook)
1. Sanitation workers—Fiction. 2. Refuse and refuse disposal—Fiction.
3. Graphic novels. I. Title.
  PN6727.D466T73 2015
  741.5'973—dc23
                        2015011115

Printed and bound in the United States
10 9 8 7 6 5 4 3 2 1

Abrams ComicArts books are available at special discounts when purchased in quan-
tity for premiums and promotions as well as fundraising or educational use. Special
editions can also be created to specification. For details, contact specialsales@abrams-
books.com or the address below.

THE ART OF BOOKS SINCE 1949
115 West 18th Street
New York, NY 10011
www.abramsbooks.com

Contents

M y first *Trashed* stories were memoir, the tale of my time as a garbageman in 1979 and 1980. These were published as a fifty-page floppy comic book in 2002. It was my first attempt at long-form comics storytelling. I also received my first Eisner nomination for the *Trashed* floppy, so it's always been a special project for me.

I returned to *Trashed* in 2010. I decided to experiment with a webcomic, and thought a new *Trashed* would be a fun venture in this format. I did one forty-page *Trashed* story in 2010, then another installment in 2011. But as I worked on the narrative it became clear this was no longer a memoir. I brought the story up to the present day and decided to make it fiction. Portions of this book are taken from those two webcomics. This book is inspired by my experiences, but none of the characters or places are real.

Thanks to my beloved editor, Charlie Kochman, for suggesting this book, and to my awesome agent, Matthew Carnicelli. You guys are the best.

Thanks also to Pam Notarantonio, who designed and colored the cover and babysat this book all the way to print.

And to Jen Graham, who copyedited my shoddy prose and saved me from misspelling every word longer than two syllables.

Thanks to my old pal Mike, who made that year on the truck bearable.

Thanks to all the fans and readers around the globe who have made my late-career reboot as a graphic novelist so fabulous.

This book is dedicated to my wife, Sheryl, who suffered nobly as a "comix widow" for the fourteen months it took me to make it. She is, as she so often reminds me, my muse.

derf
Derf Backderf
Shaker Heights, Ohio
June 2015

OK, YOU. IT'S NOON. YOU **CAN'T** SNOOZE THE DAY AWAY.

IT'S **GARBAGE PICKUP** TODAY. PUT THE CANS OUT, PLEASE.

AND **HERE'S** A TRASH BAG. PICK UP **ALL** THE GARBAGE AND OLD FOOD IN HERE.

GROAN. C'MON, MA.

I DON'T KNOW **HOW** YOU CAN LIVE IN THIS **FILTH.**

HOW DID IT GO AT **THE MALL** YESTERDAY?

WASTE OF TIME. **NO ONE** IS HIRING.

WELL, TRY SOMEPLACE **ELSE** THEN. IT'S BEEN ALMOST **A MONTH** SINCE YOU DROPPED OUT OF COLLEGE. YOU **KNOW** OUR DEAL.

IF YOU'RE NOT GOING TO SCHOOL, YOU NEED TO BE **WORKING.**

YEAH, YEAH.

GARBAGE!

I KNOW!

GRUMBLE. MUTTER.

OOF.

A BRIEF HISTORY OF GARBAGE

TRASH DISPOSAL HAS BEEN A HEADACHE SINCE MAN FIRST BEGAN LIVING IN SETTLEMENTS.

AND THERE IS EVIDENCE THAT **ANCIENT MAN** GENERATED EVEN MORE GARBAGE ON A DAILY BASIS THAN **MODERN MAN!**

WHEN SETTLEMENTS GREW INTO **CITIES**, THE GARBAGE PROBLEM BECAME A CRISIS. THAT'S WHEN OUR FORE-FATHERS INVENTED...

...THE DUMP! THE FIRST ONE DATES TO 3000 B.C. IN THE CITY OF KNOSSOS ON CRETE.

BUT MOSTLY PEOPLE JUST LIVED WITH THEIR GARBAGE. THE FAVORITE METHOD OF DISPOSAL WAS TO SIMPLY **TOSS IT** OUT THE WINDOW ONTO THE STREET, WHERE IT WOULD ROT AND REEK.

LVTETIA VRBS PARISIORVM

In the 1400s, **THE PILES** of stinking garbage outside the walls of Paris were so high, city defenses were compromised.

Finally, after 4,000-plus years of living knee-deep in their own filth, our ancestors decided there **MUST** be a better way.

It was the English who developed Europe's first highly efficient method of trash collection and recycling.

By the 1800s, a legion of **'DUST MEN'** collected all refuse in London. Everything was sorted in huge yards on the outskirts of the city.

Nearly **100 PERCENT** of London's waste was reused or recycled. It's the same principle we still employ.

BENJAMIN FRANKLIN was America's sanitation pioneer. He formed the first street-cleaning force in Philadelphia in 1792.

Philadelphia's trash was hauled out of the city by slaves, who dumped it into the Delaware River downstream.

IN PRE-CIVIL WAR AMERICA, THE COMMON SOLUTION TO GARBAGE ON CITY STREETS **WAS PIGS.** NEW YORK CITY HAD **SO MANY** FREE-ROAMING HOGS THAT **CHARLES DICKENS** IN "AMERICAN NOTES" BEGGED CITY FATHERS TO RID THE METROPOLIS OF THE "UGLY BRUTES."

TRASH COLLECTION AS A FUNCTION OF GOVERNMENT DIDN'T BECOME COMMONPLACE UNTIL THE 1880s.

CITY OF CLEVELAND

BY 1900, CITIES DECIDED THAT **BURNING TRASH** WAS THE BEST METHOD OF DISPOSAL. BUT THE MUNICIPAL **INCINERATORS** WERE POORLY DESIGNED AND DIFFICULT TO MAINTAIN. MOST WERE SCRAPPED BY 1920.

AFTER WORLD WAR II, LANDFILLS WERE THE NEAR-UNIVERSAL DESTINATION FOR THE NATION'S TRASH. OFTEN COMMUNITIES WOULD "RECLAIM" WETLANDS. DUMPS WERE LARGELY UNREGULATED. NOT UNTIL 1979 DID THE E.P.A. ISSUE RULES ON HOW LANDFILLS WERE BUILT AND OPERATED.

FROM 1960 ON, HOUSEHOLD WASTE IN THE U.S. INCREASED DRAMATICALLY, AS **CONSPICUOUS CONSUMPTION** AND **BUILT-IN OBSOLESCENCE** BECAME THE NORM. WE BECAME A **THROWAWAY SOCIETY.**

HOW MUCH GARBAGE DO WE PRODUCE? WITH THE TRASH **AMERICANS** GENERATE, THE E.P.A. ESTIMATES THAT IN **JUST 18 MONTHS,** WE *COULD* FORM A BUMPER-TO-BUMPER LINE OF FULL GARBAGE TRUCKS THAT WOULD STRETCH ALL THE WAY TO **THE MOON!** **EUROPEANS** AREN'T MUCH BETTER, AND **CANADIANS** GENERATE MORE GARBAGE PER CAPITA THAN ANYONE ON EARTH!

17

18

23

HEY! A PARKING SPACE FOR ONCE! USUALLY WE HAVE TO PARK BEHIND **THE MULCH SHED** OUT BACK.

RRRR

A GOOD OMEN.

AND A RARE CRACK IN THE **CASTE SYSTEM** OF THE VILLAGE GOVERNMENT. THE **SALARIED GUYS** GET ALL THE PERKS...

...PARKING SPACES, FREE WORK UNIFORMS, BENEFITS, DECENT PAY. JUST LOOK AT THE **EXPENSIVE CARS** THEY ALL DRIVE.

WHILE US **"HOURLY WORKERS"** GET SQUAT! EVEN THOUGH WE WORK THE SAME 40-HOUR WEEK.

BUDGET LINE SUBTERFUGE!

GUESS THEY FIGURE ONLY **A FOOL** WOULD PUT UP WITH THIS INEQUALITY FOR **LONG**...

THEY **UNDER-ESTIMATE** US!

WHAT KILLS ME IS THAT EVERYONE THINKS WE MAKE **BIG MONEY** BECAUSE WE'RE GARBAGEMEN!

YEAH.

LIKE **UNION** GUYS IN A BIG CITY.

WHEN, OF COURSE, **THE REALITY** IS...

YOU'RE LATE!

GUS IS A REAL PIECE OF WORK. A MACHO, HARD-ASS SHRIMP WHO CONSTANTLY BRAGS OF HIS SEXUAL CONQUESTS. **SHORT** IN STATURE, **BIG** IN DOUCHEBAGGERY.

LOOKIT **THIS** PAIR!

DIRK IS THE KIND OF MUSCLE-BOUND ADONIS WHO SCARED THE **CRAP** OUT OF ME IN SCHOOL. TURNS OUT HE'S A GOOD GUY. I HATE IT WHEN MY FEARS DON'T HOLD UP.

YEAH.

WOODY, YOU'VE GOT THE PARK.

RIGHT.

THIS GUY...WHAT A **SLEAZY** DUDE. HAS ALL SORTS OF SKETCHY SIDE OPERATIONS, **AND** HE'S A **TOTAL CROOK.**

HE'S ALSO A **CLASS-A RACIST** BUT...HE'S A **RELATIVE** OF WILE E....

...SO HE'S SAFE.

ROAD CREW, START ON SANFORD ROAD.

THE SUMMER HELP. COLLEGE GUYS.

OK.

CURT, YOU'VE GOT TREE PLANTING.

CUUUUURTIS!

CURTIS INTERRUPTUS!

KNOCK IT OFF!

HEH. CURT. **SUCH** A SMART-ASS. HE'S GOOD AT THE JOB, THOUGH. **HE AND DIRK** ARE THE ONLY ONES WHO KEEP THIS TOWN FROM TOTAL RUIN.

MORONS.

BONE, THE PACKER IS GOOD TO GO AGAIN.

RIGHTO.

POOR **"BONE."** BOB REPUTEDLY HAS A **GENIUS I.Q.,** BUT HE LIVES WITH HIS **MOM** AND DRIVES A **GARBAGE TRUCK.**

TAKE IT EASY, OK? YOU REALLY **MANGLED** THAT WHEEL.

SORRY.

GARBAGE! ACCORDING TO THE E.P.A., AMERICANS PRODUCE **254 MILLION TONS** OF IT A YEAR.

WE PUT IT OUT ON THE CURB EVERY WEEK AND, WHILE WE'RE AT WORK OR SCHOOL, SOMEONE **TAKES IT AWAY.**

PROBLEM SOLVED! NO MORE GARBAGE!

RRRRR

BUT IN REALITY, ALL THAT STINKING, ROTTING GARBAGE HAS TO GO **SOME**WHERE. IT DOESN'T, IN FACT, JUST VANISH.

THE E.P.A. CALCULATES THAT **EACH AMERICAN** — MAN, WOMAN, CHILD, AND BABE IN ARMS — MAKES **2.89 POUNDS OF TRASH** EACH AND EVERY DAY. THAT'S THE TOTAL **AFTER** RECYCLING AND COMPOSTING.

THE E.P.A.'S RECORDS SHOW THAT IN 1960, EACH OF US TOSSED OUT **2.51 POUNDS OF GARBAGE,** AFTER RECYCLING, WHICH WAS ALMOST NONEXISTENT THEN. SO TODAY WE RECYCLE **34.3 PERCENT** OF OUR TRASH AND **STILL** SEND MORE TO THE LANDFILL EVERY DAY.

YES, OUR DAILY TOTAL IS ONLY **SLIGHTLY MORE** THAN IT WAS OVER FOUR DECADES AGO. ONLY ONE PROBLEM. IN 1960, THE U.S. POPULATION WAS ONLY **181 MILLION.** TODAY THERE'S OVER **321 MILLION** OF US!

THE GRIM REALITY IS THAT EACH OF US NOW GENERATES **MORE TRASH,** AND THERE'S **ALMOST TWICE AS MANY OF US!**

AND HERE'S ANOTHER PROBLEM: THESE E.P.A. NUMBERS ARE LIKELY A RIDICULOUS **UNDER**ESTIMATE!

SO WHAT EXACTLY **IS** OUR GARBAGE? AS OF THIS WRITING, **THE E.P.A.** LAST ANALYZED OUR 2013 MUNICIPAL WASTE. ALL THESE FIGURES COME FROM THAT REPORT.

HERE'S WHAT MAKES UP **OUR TRASH...**

AAAAUGH!

SCREEE!!

14.6 PERCENT OF IT IS FOOD SCRAPS. **13.5 PERCENT** IS YARD WASTE.

ASSHOLES!

SMELLY STUFF, BUT ALL **BIODEGRADABLE**. IT BREAKS DOWN INTO COMPOST.

20.3 PERCENT IS WHAT THE E.P.A. LABELS **DURABLE GOODS**: APPLIANCES, TIRES, FURNITURE, RUGS, ETC. THESE MATERIALS **CAN** BE RECYCLED BUT OFTEN **AREN'T**.

FOR EXAMPLE, **32.5 MILLION TONS OF PLASTIC** IS THROWN AWAY ANNUALLY. ONLY **9.2 PERCENT** OF THAT IS RECYCLED. THAT'S ALL!

SO FAR, THAT ACCOUNTS FOR **48.4 PERCENT** OF OUR HOUSEHOLD TRASH...

OF THE REMAINING REFUSE, **20.3 PERCENT** IS WHAT THE E.P.A. CALLS **NONDURABLE GOODS**: ITEMS THAT ARE USED ONCE, THEN THROWN AWAY, SUCH AS CLEANING WIPES, AND DISPOSABLE DIAPERS...

ICK. DIAPER BAGS. **HOW** MANY DAMN KIDS DO THESE PEOPLE **HAVE**?

THE AVERAGE CHILD WILL GO THROUGH UP TO **8,000 DIAPERS** BEFORE BEING POTTY TRAINED! THAT TOTALS **18 BILLION** (THAT'S **BILLION!**) POOPY DIAPERS HEADING TO U.S. LANDFILLS EACH AND EVERY YEAR.

THE HOPPER IS **FULL**. "CYCLE" IT, MAN.

THE GOOD NEWS IS, **31.8 PERCENT** OF NONDURABLE GOODS IS **COMPOSTED** OR **RECYCLED**.

CYCLING.

NOT, HOWEVER, THE DIAPERS.

CLICK!

CYCLE

2

3   4

STOP

RRRRRRR

CREEEEEAK!

RRRᴀʀʀʀʀRRR

CHUNK!

WHIIIIIIIIRRR

CREEEEK!

AND THE REMAINING **29.8 PERCENT** OF OUR GARBAGE? IT'S **PACKAGING AND CONTAINERS.**

THAT'S RIGHT. THE **LARGEST PART** OF OUR CRAP IS THE CRAP OUR CRAP COMES IN*!*

RRRRRRRR

HEADS UP!

DIAPER BOMBS!

BLAM! BLAM!

AAAA!

SPLAT!

SPLAT!

THUD!

SPLAT!

AWWWW, **MAN!**

HA! DIRECT HIT!

ICK.

WELL, **DON'T** STAND IN BETTY'S **LINE OF FIRE,** YOU FOOL.

THIS IS TH' **LAST** OF IT.

THAT'S OUR TRASH.

RRRRRRRR

BUT...THE E.P.A.'S FIGURE OF **2.89 POUNDS OF TRASH DAILY** IS **WAY** LOW. AN INDEPENDENT BIANNUAL STUDY BY **COLUMBIA UNIVERSITY** FINDS OUR ANNUAL GARBAGE TOTAL **ISN'T** 254 MILLION TONS... IT'S **389 MILLION TONS!** AND WE RECYCLE ONLY **29 PERCENT,** NOT THE 34.3 PERCENT THE E.P.A. CLAIMS.

THE TRUTH? EACH OF US MAKES **5.06 POUNDS OF GARBAGE** A DAY. NO BIG DEAL, RIGHT? THAT **DOESN'T** SEEM LIKE MUCH...

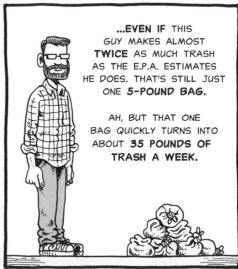

...**EVEN IF** THIS GUY MAKES ALMOST **TWICE** AS MUCH TRASH AS THE E.P.A. ESTIMATES HE DOES. THAT'S STILL JUST ONE **5-POUND BAG.**

AH, BUT THAT ONE BAG QUICKLY TURNS INTO ABOUT **35 POUNDS OF TRASH A WEEK.**

HMMM.

AND ROUGHLY **150 POUNDS A MONTH.**

AND **1,847 POUNDS A YEAR!**

365 SMALL BAGS MAKE **QUITE** A PILE, NO?

YIKES!

33

IT'S **DOVER**, THE FIRE CHIEF, **"LIPS" McCOY**, OUR BELOVED SERVICE DIRECTOR, AND **STIVCHEK**, THE POLICE CHIEF...

IT'S THE **ENTIRE** FRIGGIN' TOWN GOVERNMENT...AND THEY'RE JUST STANDING IN FRONT OF THE DRUGSTORE **STARING AT US!**

WHAT TH' HELL DID WE DO **WRONG** NOW?

LET'S SPLIT BEFORE WE FIND OUT. **OK, BONE!**

WEIRD.

LOOK.

SCREE!

THIS GUY PUT OUT HIS **OLD STOVE** AGAIN. THIRD WEEK IN A ROW.

HEY!

RRRRR

NOW, LOOK...

I KEEP **HAULING** THIS DAMN STOVE OUT HERE, AND YOU GUYS KEEP **LEAVING** IT. **WHAT'S** TH' DEAL?

WE ONLY TAKE APPLIANCES ON **HEAVY TRASH DAY.** VILLAGE RULES. SORRY.

WHEN'S THE **NEXT** HEAVY TRASH DAY?

MARCH.

WHAT?

AW, C'MON.

APPLIANCES FILL US UP **TOO FAST.**

MAN, IT **IS** HEAVY.

TELL YA **WHAT...**

CREEEAK!

THUMP!

IF YOU TAKE **THE DOORS** OFF, WE CAN PICK **THOSE** UP WHEN WE PASS BY AGAIN LATER TODAY.

CREAK!

THAT'S **ALL?** THE DOORS?

YEP.

AND YOU'LL HAVE TO GET IT OFF THE CURB BY TOMORROW **OR** YOU'LL GET A TICKET.

AAAARGH!

YOU HAVE A **NICE DAY**, SIR.

RRRRR

ANOTHER HAPPY VILLAGER.

WE'RE HERE TO **SERVE**.

RRRRR

THE **ONLY** GOOD THING ABOUT THIS JOB...

...IS THE **FUN** OF **DISAPPOINTING** THE PUBLIC!

OW!

SPLAT!

ZZZIP!

39

SCRUNCH!

AAAAAR!

RIIIP!

DAMMIT!

THAT'S THE **THIRD** BAG THAT'S **SPLIT APART** TODAY!

TH' **GROCERY** MUSTA SWITCHED TO A **CHEAPER** GENERIC BRAND.

I **HATE** IT WHEN IT GETS INTO MY BOOT THROUGH THE LACES!

HANG ON. I'LL GET **THE SHOVEL.**

DON'T BOTHER.

OK, LET'S ROLL.

42

44

RRR RRR

HE'S CHASING IT **RIGHT INTO** SMITH'S ORCHARD!

RRRRRR

THAT OLD COOT IS **NUTS!**

MR. WATCHDOG SHOULD GET STUFF LIKE **THAT** ON FILM!

MAYBE HE'S **NOT** A LOON AFTER ALL! **KEEP ROLLING**, MR. WATCHDOG.

HUP.

WHAT TH'...? OH, **HERE'S** ONE FOR THE BOOKS!

SCREE!

CHECK IT OUT.

THESE CLOWNS PUT OUT THE **CAT BOX.** DIDN'T EMPTY IT. SET IT ON THE CAN...

...WITH **THE CAT!** **DECEASED!**

EW!

TOUGH DAY FOR PETS IN THIS TOWN.

HOW **VERY** TOUCHING.

POOR KITTY.

HEY, IT'S HOW **I** WANT TO GO!

UH-OH.

WILE E. IS GOING TO **FREAK** ABOUT THIS. BETTER RADIO HIM.

LET'S EAT **BEFORE** OLD MAN JONES DISCOVERS WE **BROKE** HIS STORE. **BLT**, BONE?

YOU **GOTTA** STOP RUNNING INTO STUFF, MAN.

SIGH.

I'LL GET IT **TO** GO.

YEAH.

POOR BONE. FOR A GUY WHO'S **ÜBER SMART**, HE **SURE** IS A **SCREWUP**.

IS IT **TRUE** BOB'S NICKNAME IS...?

...**BECAUSE** OF THE **ENORMITY** OF HIS **MANHOOD**? THAT'S THE LEGEND.

YOU'LL NOTICE HE **DOESN'T** PROTEST WHEN WE CALL HIM "BONE."

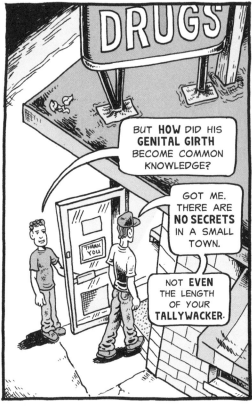

DRUGS

BUT **HOW** DID HIS **GENITAL GIRTH** BECOME COMMON KNOWLEDGE?

GOT ME. THERE ARE **NO SECRETS** IN A SMALL TOWN.

NOT **EVEN** THE LENGTH OF YOUR **TALLYWACKER**.

THANK YOU

WELL, **THIS** MORNING... GIGGLE...THE COFFEE MACHINE **BROKE!**

WHAT? **HA!!**

THEY'RE **PROBABLY** ALL BACK AT TOWN HALL, WITH THEIR HEADS ON THEIR DESKS, **UNCAFFEINATED AND HELPLESS!**

ALL THAT STANDS BETWEEN US AND **TOTAL ANARCHY** IS ONE CRANKY **MR. COFFEE MACHINE!**

OH **MAN.** IT'S BETH HODL!

HMM?

BETH! HAVEN'T SEEN **YOU** IN A WHILE.

UH...?

IT'S J.B.! WE SAT **NEXT** TO EACH OTHER IN **HOMEROOM...**

...FOR **SIX** YEARS.

OH! GOSH, I DIDN'T EVEN **RECOGNIZE** YOU!

WHAT HAVE **YOU** BEEN UP TO?

WORKING FOR **THE VILLAGE** RIGHT NOW.

WENT TO **COLLEGE** FOR A BIT. MIGHT GO BACK **EVENTUALLY.**

COOL. **WHAT** DO YOU—SNIFF—DO FOR THE VILLAGE?

THIS AND THAT. WE WORK IN **THE SERVICE DEPART...**

...WE'RE YOUR **GARBAGEMEN.**

THAT—SNIFF— **EXPLAINS** IT.

WELL, HEY, **NICE** TO SEE YOU AGAIN.

HERE'S YOUR **SANDWICH**, BONE. YA OWE ME THREE BUCKS.

THANKS.

HOW **BAD** DID WILE E. REAM YOU?

'BOUT TH' **USUAL**.

READY FOR...**THE HEIGHTS?**

UGH. THAT HILLBILLY NEIGHBORHOOD IS **THE PITS!**

OMIGOD! I **DON'T** BELIEVE IT!

IT'S ONE OF THE **APPLE-TOSSING CREEPS** FROM THIS MORNING!

I RECOGNIZE HIS **CHEESY SHIRT.**

TH-THAT'S NOT THE APPLE-THROWING KID! HE DIDN'T WEAR G-GLASSES!

WAAA!

WHAT HAVE I DONE? I-I-I JUST THREW TRASH ALL OVER AN INNOCENT CHILD!

HAHAHAHA! OH, YOU COLOSSAL DUMBASS!

PRAY NO ONE WITNESSED THAT!

THE LITTLE BUGGER IS JUST WALKING ALONG ON A SUMMER DAY AND—POW! BOMBED WITH CRAP!

HA!

AND HE'LL NEVER KNOW WHY!

YEAH, WELL... GET USED TO IT, KID!

IT'S A GLIMPSE OF...SNORT!... WHAT AWAITS YOU IN LIFE!

NO ONE WILL BELIEVE THE POOR GUY. HE'LL GO HOME COVERED IN FILTH AND TELL HIS MOM HE WAS ATTACKED BY GARBAGE-MEN, AND HE'LL PROBABLY BE GROUNDED FOR LYING!

HA HA!

HA HA HA HA HA!

HA HA HA ACK!

ZZZZZZZZZ

GAG! CHOKE! HACK!

64

THE LAST STOP! THE RUN, SHE IS **FINITO!**

WHEW.

RRRRRR

SCREE!

WHAT'S BONE **STOPPING** FOR? WE **ALREADY DID** THIS STREET.

HA.

OUR **UNHAPPY VILLAGER** WITH **THE STOVE**...HE TOOK OFF **THE DOORS,** AS INSTRUCTED.

HEY, LOOK.

GIMME A HAND WITH THE "PICKS" I STASHED IN THE CAB, WILLYA?

SEE YA TOMORROW, BONE.

BYE, GUYS.

GROAN. MAN! I AM TOTALLY WHIPPED.

MAGEE! OPEN UP! MY HANDS ARE FULL! MAGEE!

BANG! BANG!

GRR!

I KNOW YOU'RE IN HERE, YOU REDHEADED MANIAC. TH' PLACE REEKS OF THOSE IDIOTIC CLOVE CIGARETTES OF YOURS.

WHERE'S THE...OOF... LIGHT SWITCH...?

PORN ALERT!

QUITE A STASH. MAGS...OLD VHS TAPES...

REAL **HARDCORE STUFF**...YIK.

SAY, **ISN'T** THIS...? **IT IS!** HEY, MIKE!

WANNA KNOW **THE PORN HABITS** OF YOUR **MATH TEACHER?**

WHY DO PEOPLE PUT THAT STUFF OUT ON THE CURB **LIKE THAT?**

DO THEY THINK WE **WON'T NOTICE?**

MORE LIKELY THEY DON'T THINK ABOUT US **AT ALL!**

WE **DON'T EXIST.** TRASH DISAPPEARS... **LIKE MAGIC!**

RRRRR (GROAN!)

RATS. **ALMOST FULL.** WE'LL HAVE TO HIT **THE DUMP** AFTER LUNCH.

YEAH! HE PRETENDS HE'S THE **GREAT WHITE HUNTER**...

...WHEN, IN REALITY, HE'S THE **GREAT WHITE DISTRACTED DRIVER!**

WHUMP!

WAIT UNTIL THE HOPPER IS **FULL** BEFORE CYCLING. IT'S **GROSS** WHEN A DEER BODY GETS **CHEWED UP.**

UGH. ROTTEN **JACK-O'-LANTERNS.**

SKY HOOK!

SPLOT!

HOLIDAYS ARE A **DRAG.** AND NEXT UP IS THE WORST ONE: **THANKSGIVING!** THE RACCOONS GO **MEDIEVAL** ON EVERY CAN WITH A **TURKEY CARCASS!**

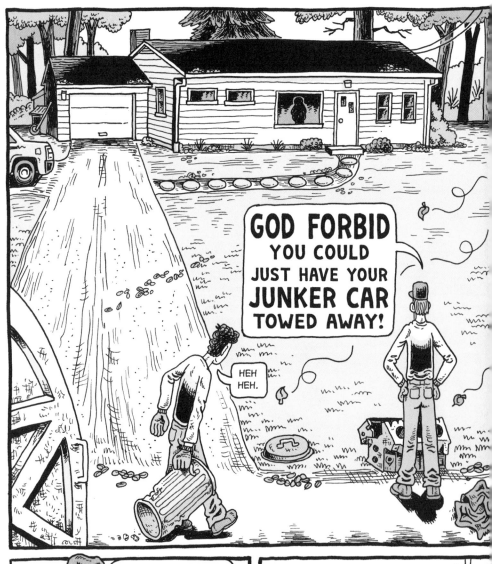

GOD FORBID YOU COULD JUST HAVE YOUR JUNKER CAR TOWED AWAY!

HEH HEH.

INSTEAD, HE CHOPS IT UP AND PUTS IT OUT FOR THE TRASH —PIECE BY PIECE!— ALL YEAR LONG!

LOOK AT HIM! WATCHING FROM HIS WINDOW TO MAKE SURE WE TAKE IT ALL AND LEAVE NOTHING BEHIND!

EVERY WEEK!

AND SINCE HE **BITCHES** WHEN WE LEAVE SOMETHING, OUR FEARLESS SERVICE DIRECTOR, "LIPS" McCOY, HAS ORDERED US TO **TAKE IT ALL.** THAT WAY, LIPS'S **THREE-HOUR LUNCH** WON'T BE **INTERRUPTED.**

SOOOO...

OK, LET'S **DO** THIS.

GOOD MAN, BONE.

OH, SWEET **MOTHER OF GOD!!**

GRUNT!

SCRAPE!

I WONDER IF **WALMART** IS HIRING NIGHTTIME BAG BOYS?

HEY! ONE-BAGGER!

SWEET! ONE-BAGGERS ARE CIVIC TREASURES!

RRR

RRR

82

83

RECYCLING. IT'S TOUTED AS **THE SOLUTION** TO OUR TRASH PROBLEM, AND AMERICANS HAVE TAKEN TO IT IN **IMPRESSIVE** NUMBERS. WE RECYCLE **29 PERCENT** OF OUR 389 MILLION ANNUAL TONS OF GARBAGE. BUT IS IT **REALLY** DOING ANY GOOD?

THE RESULTS ARE MIXED.

MOST COMMUNITIES HAVE **SOME** CURBSIDE RECYCLING. IT VARIES GREATLY. **BIG CITIES** TEND TO RUN THEIR OWN RECYCLING OPERATION. **SMALLER TOWNS** USUALLY FARM IT OUT TO PRIVATE COMPANIES.

HEY, IT'S THE **RECYCLING GUYS.**

GOODY.

HIYA, GENTS! WOW, THAT'S **SOME** PILE!

TELL ME ABOUT IT.

RATTLE! CLINK!

WE RECYCLE

TINKLE! KRASH! TINK!

THE MOST EFFECTIVE PROGRAM WITH THE HIGHEST PARTICIPATION RATE IS **SINGLE-STREAM RECYCLING.** ALL MATERIALS ARE PLACED IN THE SAME BIN AND SEPARATED AT A FACILITY. AMERICANS **LIKE** THE IDEA OF RECYCLING—OUR RECYCLING RATE HAS ROUGHLY **DOUBLED** SINCE 1990— BUT WE **DON'T** LIKE THE PROCESS TO BE INCONVENIENT.

BUT EVEN WITH A **DRAMATIC RISE** IN RECYCLING, IT'S ONLY MADE A SLIGHT DENT OVER THE SAME PERIOD OF TIME IN THE STAGGERING AMOUNT OF GARBAGE WE SEND TO THE LANDFILL EACH YEAR.

BUT THERE'S **BIG MONEY** IN RECYCLING, RIGHT? NOT REALLY. IT DEPENDS ON **THE PRICE** RECYCLED MATERIALS FETCH ON THE COMMODITIES MARKET, AND THOSE **HAVEN'T** BEEN HIGH ENOUGH TO MAKE RECYCLING PROFITABLE. AT LEAST TOWNS GET **SOMETHING** TO OFFSET THE COST OF COLLECTION, AS OPPOSED TO TRASH PICKUP, WHICH IS JUST AN OUTRIGHT EXPENS...AND **A GROWING ONE.**

SURE, RECYCLING ALL WE CAN IS THE **COMMONSENSE THING** TO DO—WHY ENTOMB RESOURCES IN A LANDFILL?—BUT IT'S **NOT** THE ANSWER TO OUR GARBAGE PROBLEM. THAT SOLUTION IS: USE **LESS STUFF** IN THE FIRST PLACE!

WHEW! WORKING UP **A SWEAT** HERE!

AND **THAT'S** THE UNSOLVABLE QUANDARY. ARE WE GOING TO **GIVE UP** OUR PLASTIC DRINK BOTTLES, DISPOSABLE DIAPERS, AND PLASTIC SHOPPING BAGS?

YOU **KNOW** THE ANSWER.

BOINK!

OK. THIS IS **THE LAST** OF IT.

FINALLY!

COLLECTION OF RECYCLABLES VARIES GREATLY, TOO. SOME CREWS SORT THE MATERIALS AS THEY PICK THEM UP — GLASS IN ONE HOPPER, METAL IN ANOTHER, ETC. — WHILE OTHERS JUST TOSS IT ALL IN ONE HOPPER.

TRUCKS DEPOSIT THEIR LOADS AT A **MATERIALS RECOVERY FACILITY,** WHERE RECYCLABLES ARE **SEPARATED** AND **PROCESSED.**

MATERIALS ARE THEN **CRUSHED** OR **SHREDDED** AND THEN BAILED UP FOR **RESALE** TO INDUSTRY...

SOME FACILITIES ARE MOSTLY **AUTOMATED,** OTHERS SORT MATERIALS **BY HAND,** AND SOME EMPLOY A COMBINATION OF METHODS.

PRETTY CRAPPY JOB, BUT OVERALL, WORKING IN **THE RECYCLING BIZ** IS A DANCE THROUGH THE TULIPS COMPARED TO TRASH **PICKUP.**

94

JUST TRYING IT ON FOR SIZE.

DROP THIS OFF AT THE SHOP FOR ME. I'LL SAVE TH' VILLAGE A FEW SHEKELS IN DUMPING FEES.

DON'T SCRATCH THE BED!

YOU GUYS WILL HAVE TO INTERRUPT YOUR RUN. THERE'S A BRUSH PILE OVER ON HARPER ROAD...

VILLAGE SERVICE DEPT.

HOOK UP THE CHIPPER TO TRUCK THREE AND TAKE CARE OF IT.

OK.

RRRRRRR
CREEAAK!

I LOVE THAT GUY!

RRRR

BETTY IS FULL! THE FORECLOSURE PILE DID IT.

THE GARBAGE TRUCK HAS BEEN ON THE STREETS FOR ALMOST 100 YEARS, BUT ITS BASIC DESIGN HAS CHANGED VERY LITTLE.

THE FIRST TRUCKS WERE **MODIFIED MODEL Ts.** IT WAS SIMPLY A MOTORIZED VERSION OF THE HORSE-DRAWN GARBAGE WAGON THAT HAD BEEN IN USE FOR CENTURIES. THE MODEL Ts DIDN'T HOLD MUCH OF A LOAD, AND GARBAGEMEN HAD TO HOIST HEAVY CANS OVER THEIR HEADS.

1934 REFUSE COMPRESSOR
from **MARION METAL PRODUCTS**

THE FIRST BIG ADVANCE IN TRUCK DESIGN CAME WHEN MARION METAL INVENTED **THE PACKER.** AN INTERIOR METAL PLATE, POWERED BY HYDRAULICS, PACKED TRASH IN THE HOLD. BY COMPRESSING THE LOAD, A TRUCK COULD HOLD THREE TIMES MORE GARBAGE BEFORE HEADING TO THE DUMP. EFFICIENCY WAS SIGNIFICANTLY INCREASED.

1919 FORD MODEL T GARBAGE TRUCK

HOW A TRUCK LIKE BETTY WORKS

IT'S ACTUALLY QUITE SIMPLE...

FREE-MOVING INTERNAL BLADE PREVENTS TRASH FROM SPILLING BACK INTO THE HOPPER.

THE TAILGATE BLADE SWEEPS TRASH OUT OF THE HOPPER, PACKING IT TIGHTLY IN THE HOLD.

TRASH IS COMPACTED BY THE TWIN FORCE OF THE TAILGATE BLADE AND THE COMPRESSION PLATE.

THE PACKER ALSO INTRODUCED THE ENCLOSED HOLD. THIS GREATLY REDUCED SMELLS AND SPILLS. AT THE DUMP, THE COMPRESSION PLATE ALSO EJECTED THE GARBAGE LOAD OUT A BACK HATCH. BOTH OF THESE FEATURES ARE STILL THE NORM TODAY.

1938 GARWOOD LOAD PACKER

THE REAR-LOADING PACKER WAS DEVELOPED BY GARWOOD. IT REVOLUTIONIZED TRASH PICKUP BY COMBINING THE PACKER WITH A LOW HOPPER THAT MADE IT EASIER FOR GARBAGEMEN TO EMPTY CANS. WHEN THE HOPPER WAS FULL, A POWERFUL TAILGATE BLADE SWEPT THE TRASH UP INTO THE INTERNAL HOLD, WHERE IT WAS PACKED. IT WAS SUCH AN EFFECTIVE AND EFFICIENT DESIGN, IT IS STILL THE STANDARD MORE THAN 75 YEARS LATER.

THE GARWOOD AND ITS MANY IMITATORS BECAME AN ALMOST UNIVERSAL CHOICE FOR MUNICIPAL GARBAGE COLLECTION BY 1960. MORE THAN A MILLION OF THESE TYPES OF TRUCKS WERE ON THE STREETS IN AMERICAN CITIES AND TOWNS.

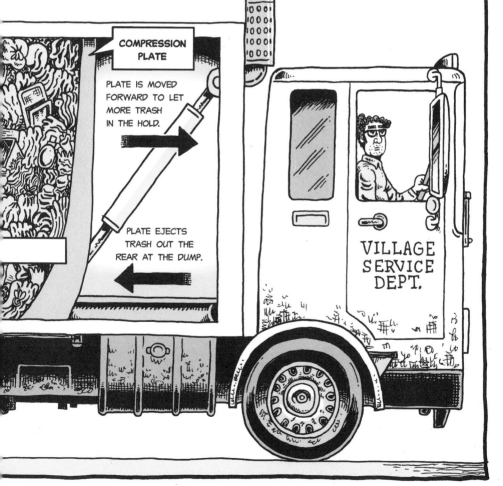

COMPRESSION PLATE

PLATE IS MOVED FORWARD TO LET MORE TRASH IN THE HOLD.

PLATE EJECTS TRASH OUT THE REAR AT THE DUMP.

VILLAGE SERVICE DEPT.

98

101

THE NUMBER OF MUNICIPAL LANDFILLS HAS **DECREASED** CONSIDERABLY OVER THE PAST FEW DECADES. THAT'S **MISLEADING,** THOUGH, AS **THE SIZE** OF THE REMAINING LANDFILLS HAS **GREATLY INCREASED.**

HOW BIG ARE OUR LANDFILLS NOW? THE E.P.A. HASN'T COMPILED THAT INFORMATION, FOR OBVIOUS POLITICAL REASONS. BUT **HERE'S** A CLUE. IN 2008, THE **SALTON CITY LANDFILL** IN SOUTHERN CALIFORNIA WAS **EIGHT ACRES.** BY 2012, IT HAD EXPANDED...**TO 287 ACRES!** AND THE DEPTH OF THE FILL WAS INCREASED FROM **45 FEET** TO **250 FEET!**

LANDFILLS

HERE'S HOW THESE THINGS ARE BUILT

1 A MODERN LANDFILL IS CONSTRUCTED OF **"CELLS,"** 50 FEET SQUARE BY 15 FEET DEEP. TRUCKS DEPOSIT THEIR FRESH LOADS ALL INTO ONE CELL, WHERE LARGE BULLDOZERS COMPRESS THE TRASH. IT'S LIKE A STACK OF GARBAGE LEGOS.

2 WHEN **A CELL IS FULL** AT THE END OF THE DAY, IT'S COVERED WITH **SIX INCHES OF DIRT** TO LIMIT THE GHASTLY SMELL AND THE BLOWING GARBAGE AND TO CONFOUND VERMIN AND BIRDS. YEAH, DOESN'T REALLY WORK AS WELL AS THE LANDFILL OPERATORS CLAIM, BUT IT IS A HUGE IMPROVEMENT OVER THE OLD METHOD OF JUST DUMPING GARBAGE IN A VAST OPEN HOLE.

BUT EVEN LANDFILLS CONSTRUCTED WITH CELLS HAVE AREAS OF EXPOSED TRASH AND PILES OF DEBRIS. IT'S **NOT** A TIDY OPERATION.

3 SO WHAT OCCURS **INSIDE** A LANDFILL? THINK ALL THAT GARBAGE DECOMPOSES INTO **HARMLESS COMPOST?** WRONG! NO LIGHT, NO CIRCULATING AIR, LITTLE DECOMPOSITION. A **DISPOSABLE DIAPER** WON'T BREAK DOWN FOR HUNDREDS OF YEARS. WE DON'T HAVE AN EXACT TIME, BECAUSE DISPOSABLE DIAPERS HAVE ONLY BEEN AROUND SINCE 1947 AND HAVEN'T **EVEN BEGUN** TO BREAK DOWN INSIDE LANDFILLS!

THE BIGGEST LANDFILL HAZARDS ARE **METHANE GAS** AND **LEAKS.** BURIED TRASH PRODUCES LARGE POCKETS OF **EXPLOSIVE METHANE GAS.** IT'S ALSO ONE OF THE WORST GREENHOUSE GASES. MOST LANDFILLS **SIPHON OUT** AND **COLLECT** THE METHANE FOR USE IN POWER GENERATION.

WHAT IS SHOWN HERE IS AN **ACTIVE LANDFILL** THAT IS 75 FEET DEEP. MUNICIPAL LANDFILLS TODAY ARE TYPICALLY 200 FEET DEEP WHEN FULL. THE BIGGEST ARE 400 FEET DEEP!

IT'S QUITE PROFITABLE. LANDFILLS PRODUCE METHANE FOR **30 TO 50 YEARS** AFTER THEY ARE FULL AND STOP ACCEPTING NEW TRASH.

4 LEAKS ARE THE BIGGER ISSUE. THE TOXIC LIQUID THAT IS SQUEEZED OUT OF BURIED TRASH IS CALLED **LEACHATE.** IT'S A MIX OF SOLVENTS, HOUSEHOLD CHEMICALS, OLD PAINT, AND FAR NASTIER (AND OFTEN ILLEGAL) STUFF THAT WINDS UP IN LANDFILLS. THIS ALL SEEPS DOWNWARD, HEADING STRAIGHT FOR **THE WATER TABLE.** MODERN LANDFILLS HAVE A TOUTED **"LINER,"** DESIGNED TO KEEP THIS CARCINOGENIC SOUP CONTAINED. THEY'RE LAUGHABLY INEFFECTIVE. THE E.P.A. DISCOVERED IN 1989 THAT **ALL** LANDFILL LINERS LEAK. **EVERY ONE!** A TEN-ACRE LANDFILL LEAKS UP TO 3,000 GALLONS OF TOXIC LEACHATE A YEAR, EASILY ENOUGH TO POISON A GROUNDWATER DRINKING SUPPLY.

THE LANDFILL LINER

A. A GEOTEXTILE STOPS TRASH FROM CLOGGING THE LEACHATE PIPE SYSTEM.

B. TWO FEET OF GRAVEL CONTAINS THE NETWORK OF PERFORATED PVC PIPES TO COLLECT LEACHATE, WHICH IS PUMPED OUT.

C. PLASTIC MEMBRANE 1/32" TO 1/8" THICK.

D. TWO FEET OF COMPACTED CLAY.

THAT'S IT! **THAT'S** THE SAFEGUARD!

THE E.P.A. CURRENTLY LISTS 1,908 ACTIVE MUNICIPAL LANDFILLS IN THE U.S. THAT TOTAL HAS DRAMATICALLY DROPPED. IN 1988, THERE WERE 7,924!

THE APEX LANDFILL, OUTSIDE LAS VEGAS, IS THE NATION'S BIGGEST, AT A STAGGERING 2,200 ACRES! THAT'S ALMOST 3.5 SQUARE MILES OF ROTTING GARBAGE!

NO MATTER HOW MANY TIMES I COME HERE, THE SHEER SCALE OF THIS PLACE ALWAYS ASTOUNDS ME!

WHEN WE'RE DOWN HERE IN THE PIT, YOU CAN'T EVEN SEE THE OUTSIDE WORLD. IT'S LIKE WE'RE ON A PLANET OF TRASH!

C'MON. LET'S **GET OUT** OF THIS DUMP.

JUST A SEC.

THIS **ONLY** DESCRIBES LANDFILLS STARTED IN THE **PAST 26 YEARS**...AND PRIOR TO 1979, THERE WERE **FEW REGULATIONS** AND **LITTLE MONITORING** OF LANDFILLS, EITHER BY THE FEDS OR THE STATES. THEY WERE JUST **BIG HOLES** INTO WHICH ANY AND ALL TRASH WAS DUMPED. MANY ARE **STILL** IN OPERATION.

RRRRRRRR

RATTLE! **THUMP!**

OK. WE GOTTA **PAUSE THE RUN** TO TAKE CARE OF THAT **BRUSH PILE.**

AUGH!

I **FORGOT** ABOUT THAT.

WHAT'S THE DEAL WITH THIS? WE **DON'T** PICK UP BRUSH. VILLAGERS HAVE TO **HIRE** SOMEONE.

IT'S TH' **FIRE CHIEF'S** HOUSE.

OH.

DANGIT. WE'LL **NEVER** FINISH TODAY'S RUN WITH **THIS** LITTLE DETOUR.

SO WE FINISH **TUESDAY'S** TRASH ON **WEDNESDAY.** **WHAT'S** THE DIFF?

BECAUSE...THAT MEANS THE TRASH ...IS WINNING!

AND **THAT'S** A THOUGHT I SIMPLY **CAN'T BEAR!**

AW, **MAN!** THIS'LL TAKE **ALL** AFTERNOON!

WHAT'S HE DOING? CLEAR-CUTTING **A BACKYARD AIRSTRIP?**

YES, **YARD TRIMMINGS** ARE CONSIDERED MUNICIPAL WASTE, AND WE SEND A **LOT** OF IT TO THE CURB TO BE HAULED AWAY. ALMOST **34 MILLION TONS A YEAR!** TOWNS COMPOST OR MULCH **58 PERCENT** OF THAT. YOU THINK IT WOULD BE 100 PERCENT, HUH? SO WE STILL SEND MORE THAN **14 MILLION TONS A YEAR** TO THE LANDFILL.

WHIRRR! **WHIRRR!** WHIRRR!

VROOOOM!

THE CHIPPER SCARES **THE CRAP** OUT OF ME!

ME, TOO!

LAST YEAR, SOME **POOR BUGGER**—I FORGET WHERE—GOT **TANGLED UP** IN A BRANCH AND GOT **SUCKED IN...HEAD FIRST!**

THE CORONER LISTED THE **CAUSE OF DEATH** AS **TOTAL MORSELIZATION!**

CAN YOU **BELIEVE** THAT CREEP?

GUESS WE SERFS ARE WORKING FOR **HIM** NOW, INSTEAD OF THE VILLAGE.

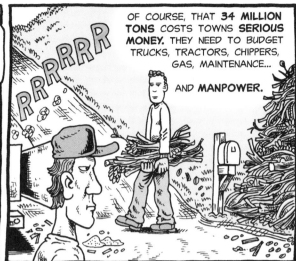

OF COURSE, THAT **34 MILLION TONS** COSTS TOWNS **SERIOUS MONEY.** THEY NEED TO BUDGET TRUCKS, TRACTORS, CHIPPERS, GAS, MAINTENANCE...

AND **MANPOWER.**

BOOOSH!

RRRRR

ZZZZZZZ

YIPE!

RRRRR

SOME TIME LATER...

OK, **THAT'S ALL** WE'RE GETTING IN THE TRUCK.

SPUTTER! SPUTTER!

LET'S **UNHOOK** THE CHIPPER AND DUMP THIS **LOAD OF MULCH** AT THE FIRST HOUSE ON THAT LIST...

UH, **BOOOOOOONE...** YOU **DO** REALIZE WE'RE ON A **VERY STEEP HILL,** RIGHT?

GRUNT!

I'LL **WAIT HERE** FOR WILE E. YOU GUYS DUMP **TH' MULCH,** THEN GET BACK ON **TH' TRASH RUN.** I'LL CATCH UP WITH YOU WHEN I **CAN.**

OK.

POOR BONE. C'MON...LET'S GET **OUT OF HERE.** I DON'T WANT TO WATCH **THE CARNAGE** ONCE WILE E. SHOWS UP!

C'MON, GEARS!

GRIND!

RRRRRRR GRIIIIIIIND!

DAMMIT!

SEVERAL MILES LATER...

LESSEE... #324...#325... **YEAH,** THIS IS **THE PLACE.**

DUMP IT **LEFT** OF THE HOUSE.

GUIDE ME IN.

I **SUCK** AT BACKING UP.

RRRR

KEEP COMING! LEFT A LITTLE!

OK, DUMP IT!

138

139

140

AT LEAST THE **WINDCHILL** ISN'T **TOO BAD**, SINCE CYCLOPS ONLY GOES FROM ZERO TO 60 IN 45 MINUTES!

THE TRASH IS ALL **TOTALLY** BURIED.

OOF! EERG! C'MON!

GET! OUTTA! **THERE!**

YEP, IT'S GONNA BE A **LOOOONG** DAY.

HALF THE CAN IS **GARBAGE SOUP**... WHICH IS **FROZEN** INTO A GIANT **TRASH CUBE!**

WHUMP!

THERE WE GO!

SCHLUP

CLUNK!

ERF!

ALL THE BAGS ARE **FROZEN** TO THE GROUND!

THAT'S 'CUZ THE BLIZZARD **STARTED** AS AN ICE STORM. **EVERYTHING** IS COATED IN ICE.

CRUNCH!

GRUNT!

WHOA!

RIIIIP!

OOF!!

THUD!

ABANDON SHIP!

SKRUNCH!

GARBAGEMAN IS THE SIXTH MOST DANGEROUS JOB IN THE U.S.!

YOU OK?

YEAH.

COPS AND FIREMEN? NOT EVEN CLOSE! ONLY LOGGERS, FISHERMEN, PILOTS, ROOFERS, AND IRONWORKERS HAVE HIGHER ON-THE-JOB FATALITY RATES.

WHIIIIIR!

RROAR! CREAK!

BUMP! WHUMP!

UH-OH. CYCLOPS TOTALLY ROACHED THAT MAILBOX.

ELABORATE CONSTRUCTION. HOMEOWNER IS OBVIOUSLY AN ANAL-RETENTIVE NUTJOB...

NOT GOOD.

GET RID OF THE OTHER BRICKS.

OBSERVE AND LEARN!

WHAT ARE YOU UP TO?

WE'LL JUST BURY THE CARCASS...

148

ANOTHER DREARY, GRAY DAY. WOTTA DRAG.

IT'S **ONLY** THE END OF FEBRUARY! WE HAVE **SIX WEEKS OF WINTER** LEFT.

AND **THEN** IT RAINS EVERY DAY FOR A MONTH.

SERVICE DEPT.

BUMP! RATTLE!

WOW. **MARV'S** HERE EARLY. **CRACK OF DAWN.** WHAT IS HE, 80-SOMETHING?

HE WAS DOGCATCHER WHEN **MY MOM** WAS A KID!

WE WERE ALL SCARED OF HIM **AS KIDS!** "MARV'S COMING FOR **YOUR DOG!**"

HEYA, MARV.

HAHA!

KOFF.

KIN **YOU** SUMBITCHES GIMME A HAND?

CAUGHT SOME **COYDOGS** LAST NIGHT.

COYDOGS?

KI-YOTES MATE WITH **STRAY DOGS.** MEAN SUMBITCHES.

WHOA! THERE'S FOUR DEAD DOGS IN HERE!

WHAT THE HELL, MARV!?!

COYDOGS. HADDA **SHOOT 'EM.** TOSS 'EM IN YER TRUCK.

KOFF.

DOG WARDEN

154

CLOSED LANDFILLS ARE A CIVIC NIGHTMARE. MOST WERE BUILT OUTSIDE CITIES, BUT, 50 YEARS LATER, THANKS TO URBAN SPRAWL, THEY'RE NOW SMACK IN THE MIDDLE OF RESIDENTIAL COMMUNITIES.

THEY'RE **EASY TO SPOT.** IF YOU DRIVE BY A LARGE AREA OF **ROLLING HILLS,** COVERED IN GRASS AND DOTTED WITH **ODD-LOOKING PIPES** STICKING OUT OF THE GROUND, **THAT'S** A CLOSED LANDFILL!

HOW MANY CLOSED LANDFILLS ARE OUT THERE? NO ONE KNOWS FOR SURE, BUT **TEXAS** DID A STUDY AND FOUND **4,200 OF THEM!**

LANDFILL CLOSED. THIS FACILITY NO LONGER ACCEPTS SOLID WASTE.

BEFORE 1979, **ANY AND EVERYTHING** WENT INTO LANDFILLS: INDUSTRIAL WASTE, PAINT, SOLVENTS, ASBESTOS, YOU NAME IT.

AND IT'S **ALL** STILL DOWN THERE.

AND THESE OLD, UNREGULATED LANDFILLS, MANY OF WHICH ARE **STILL** IN OPERATION, HAD **NONE** OF THE **MINIMAL SAFEGUARDS** OF NEWER LANDFILLS. NO LINERS, NO RUNOFF SYSTEMS TO PREVENT TOXIC LEACHATE FROM LEAKING OUT...

RRRRRRRR

ICK. EVEN **FROZEN SOLID,** THIS PLACE SMELLS LIKE **SATAN'S ASS CRACK.**

OLD OR NEW, THEY **ALL** LEAK. **EVERY** ONE. EVEN THE MOST WELL BUILT AND MAINTAINED LEAK ENOUGH **TOXIC LEACHATE** TO **RUIN** A WATER SUPPLY.

ON THE EDGE OF A CLOSED DUMP, THERE'S A **LEACHATE TANK** OR **POOL,** WHERE THE FOUL SOUP INSIDE A LANDFILL IS **SIPHONED OUT** AND COLLECTED, TO BE **TRUCKED AWAY.**

IT'S A SAFEGUARD THAT **DOESN'T** WORK. NEVER HAS, NEVER WILL.

ROAR!

AW, MAN. SOME **MORON** STASHED A BUNCH OF **OLD CHEMICALS** IN HIS BAGS! **AGAIN!** WHAT IS THAT STUFF? **INSECTICIDES?**

WHY DO PEOPLE THINK IT'S OK TO SEND THAT STUFF TO **THE DUMP?**

DON'T GET NEAR IT! IT'S PROBABLY **D.D.T.** OR **AGENT ORANGE** OR SOMETHING.

IT'S A **COMMON MISCONCEPTION** THAT, IN A DUMP, ALL TRASH QUICKLY **DECOMPOSES** INTO HARMLESS COMPOST.

A **TIN CAN** WILL TAKE **50 YEARS** TO BREAK DOWN INSIDE A LANDFILL.

THOSE **PLASTIC DRINK BOTTLES** WE LOVE SO MUCH? **450 YEARS!**

STYROFOAM? NEVER. THAT'S RIGHT. **NEVER!** POLYSTYRENE **DOESN'T** BREAK DOWN. IT MAY ERODE INTO TINY PIECES, BUT IT WON'T DECOMPOSE

THEN THERE'S THE **TOXIC SUBSTANCES.** THOSE WILL REMAIN INSIDE A LANDFILL UNTIL THEY'RE **REMOVED,** OR UNTIL THEY **ESCAPE** INTO THE ENVIRONMENT.

KICK **SOME PAMPERS** ON IT TO **SOAK IT UP!**

THE MOST DEADLY ARE **MERCURY** AND **VINYL CHLORIDE.** MERCURY COMES FROM BATTERIES, ELECTRONICS AND THOSE FLOURESCENT LIGHTBULBS WE USE TO BE MORE GREEN. MERCURY BECOMES **MORE** TOXIC WHEN BURIED.

HERE'S **ANOTHER** BAG WITH CANS OF **SOLVENT!**

PROBABLY THE **SAME** GUY...

VINYL CHLORIDE IS A GAS THAT FORMS WHEN MANUFACTURED PRODUCTS BREAK DOWN, SUCH AS INDUSTRIAL DE-GREASERS, P.V.C, UPHOLSTERY, AND EVEN KITCHEN WARE...

IT'S HIGHLY **FLAMMABLE** AND EXTREMELY **CARCINOGENIC.**

PEOPLE ARE IDIOTS!

AND THAT'S **ONLY TWO** OF THE MANY TOXIC KILLERS THAT FESTER DEEP INSIDE THOSE MOUNTAINS OF MUMMIFIED GARBAGE.

PING!

BANG!

OLD LANDFILLS ARE ECOLOGICAL TIME BOMBS...**LITERALLY.** BECAUSE, BEYOND THE TOXIC SOUP THAT LEAKS OUT THE SIDES AND BOTTOM OF A DUMP, THE BIGGEST DANGER IS **EXPLOSIVE GAS.** AS GARBAGE DECOMPOSES, IT PRODUCES LARGE UNDERGROUND POCKETS OF CARBONDIOXIDE AND METHANE GASES.

THAT'S WHAT THE PIPES ARE FOR.

THE PIPES **VENT OFF** THE GASES, WHICH PREVENTS LANDFILLS FROM ERUPTING IN **RANDOM EXPLOSIONS!** NEWER, CLOSED LANDFILLS COLLECT THE METHANE AND SELL IT OR USE IT IN ON-SITE INCINERATORS TO BURN THE TOXIC LEACHATE.

MANY OLDER LANDFILLS SIMPLY VENT GASES INTO THE AIR. LANDFILLS ACCOUNT FOR **18 PERCENT** OF MAN-MADE METHANE EMISSIONS, AND AN EQUAL AMOUNT OF CARBON DIOXIDE GAS. BOTH ARE **GREENHOUSE GASES,** METHANE BEING ONE OF THE MOST HARMFUL.

THE E.P.A. REQUIRES DUMP OWNERS TO **MONITOR AND MAINTAIN** GAS SYSTEMS FOR **30 YEARS** AFTER A LANDFILL CLOSES.

THE OLDER LANDFILLS ARE THE BIGGER WORRY. BEFORE E.P.A. RULES, ESPECIALLY IN INDUSTRIAL CITIES, LARGE QUANTITIES OF **TOXIC MATERIAL** FOUND ITS WAY INTO THESE LANDFILLS, EITHER ILLEGALLY OR BY ACCIDENT OR BY LAX OVERSIGHT. IT'S ALL **STILL** DOWN THERE, AND ALL STILL JUST AS **DEADLY.**

THIS MAKES DEVELOPING THESE LANDFILL SITES DAMN NEAR **IMPOSSIBLE,** NOT THAT SOME HAVEN'T TRIED. **SHOPPING CENTERS, OFFICE PARKS,** EVEN **APARTMENTS** HAVE BEEN BUILT ATOP CLOSED DUMPS. MANY HAVE PROVEN TO BE **DISASTERS,** SICKENING PEOPLE WHO LIVE OR WORK THERE, ALONG WITH THE OCASSIONAL METHANE FIREBALL!

SOME STATES HAVE FOUND MORE CREATIVE USES FOR OLD DUMPS, THAT LESSEN THE DANGERS TO PEOPLE. MANY HAVE BECOME **NATURE PRESERVES.** IN IOWA, ONE WAS TURNED INTO **CATTLE GRAZING LAND.**

IN WISCONSIN, A LANDFILL WAS MADE INTO **SKI SLOPES.** FLORIDA TURNED SEVERAL CLOSED DUMPS INTO—WHAT ELSE?—**GOLF COURSES.** THE **BALTIMORE ORIOLES** SPRING-TRAINING STADIUM IN SARASOTA IS BUILT ON A LANDFILL.

LOS ANGELES PLANS TO CONVERT THE JUST-CLOSED **PUENTE HILLS LANDFILL** INTO PARKS AND NATURE PRESERVES. THIS BEHEMOTH OPENED IN 1957 AND, UNTIL RECENTLY, WAS THE **BIGGEST LANDFILL IN THE U.S.** IT'S MORE THAN **500 FEET DEEP** IN PLACES AND COVERS AN AREA THE SIZE OF **CENTRAL PARK.** IT'S SO VAST, IT HAS ITS OWN **MICRO WEATHER SYSTEM!** AND SINCE IT OPERATED **FOR DECADES** BEFORE E.P.A. REGULATIONS, GOD ONLY KNOWS WHAT'S **BURIED** DEEP IN ITS BOWELS. YEAH, **GOOD LUCK** WITH **THAT** PARK.

SEVERAL STATES, SUCH AS MASSACHUSETTS, HAVE PLACED **HUGE SOLAR FARMS** ON TOP OF CLOSED DUMPS. IT'S ALMOST TRITE, RIGHT? TURNING **AN ECOLOGICAL MENACE** INTO A **GREEN ENERGY PLANT!** MAKES PERFECT SENSE, THOUGH. A SOLAR FARM NEEDS A LARGE OPEN AREA AND REQUIRES LITTLE HUMAN PRESENCE.

THAT'S IT... **QUITTIN' TIME!**

MAGEE AND I ARE GETTING **PIZZA AND BEER** AT THE PUB.

AGAIN? MAYBE I'LL STOP BY **LATER.**

RRRR

YEAH, I'M GONNA **MISS** THIS PLACE!

I DID A **QUICK TOUR** ON THE WAY IN. LOOKS LIKE **THE USUAL** OUT THERE. OH. AND **THE FORECAST** TODAY IS **RAIN** TURNING TO **SNOW**.

GROAN.

WHY IS HEAVY TRASH IN MARCH WHEN THE WEATHER IS **CRAP?**

ALWAYS **HAS** BEEN.

I'M **SURE** SUE WILL **CHANGE** IT. SHE'S HELL-BENT ON CHANGING **EVERYTHING** WE DO...

THAT STUPID WHORE!!

GEEZ.

THAT'S PRETTY **HARSH**, MAN.

WOODY, YOU TAKE **TRUCK FIVE** AND PICK UP ALL THE **ELECTRONICS, COMPUTERS, AND THE LIKE.**

CHECK.

AND HE'LL BE SELLING IT ALL ON **CRAIGSLIST** TOMORROW.

RIGHT.

GUS, DIRK, YOU'RE IN **TRUCK TWO.**

YOU GUYS HAVE **APPLIANCES.** ANYTHING WITH **COOLANT,** STACK BEHIND THE SHOP SO THE RECOVERY COMPANY CAN **DRAIN THEM.**

GOTCHA.

CURTIS, YOU AND BONE ARE ON **CYCLOPS.** PICK UP ALL **THE FURNITURE.**

OK.

MR. INTERRUPTUS!

DORKS.

YOU TWO...REGULAR TRASH, BUT TAKE **EVERY-**THING YOU CAN. **GOT IT?**

YEP.

WAITASEC...IF BONE AND CURTIS ARE ON CYCLOPS, **WHO'S** DRIVING BETTY?

YOU ARE! NO SCREW-UPS!

OH GREAT.

WE'RE A **TWO-MAN CREW** ON HEAVY TRASH DAY?

DID I SAY THAT? SUE HAS TRANSFERRED IN SOME **EXTRA MANPOWER.**

HERE HE IS NOW. **YOU'RE LATE!**

WE'RE **DOOMED!**

OK, LET'S ROLL!

THAT'S **SOME** GETUP, MAGEE.

YOU **REALLY** GONNA WEAR...

...COWBOY BOOTS?

ONLY ONES I HAVE WITH HARD TOES.

HOW DID YOU GET DRAGOONED INTO THIS, MAGEE?

DID THE HEAD GRAVE-DIGGER VOLUNTEER TO GIVE AWAY HIS LOYAL ASSISTANT?

THAT COWARD HAS HIS NOSE SO FAR UP SUE ROBINSON'S BUTT, HE CAN SMELL WHAT FLAVOR GUM SHE'S CHEWING!

VROOM!

THERE GOES THE FLEET!

RRRRR

RRR

RRRRR GRIIIND!

OK, THE MOST IMPORTANT THING...HANG ON! I DON'T WANT TO HAVE TO SCRAPE YOU OFF THE STREET LIKE A SQUASHED RACCOON.

OH, THANKS FOR THAT SECRET OF THE TRADE! HANG ON. BRILLIANT!

IT'S HARDER THAN IT SOUNDS, ESPECIALLY WITH J.B. DRIVING.

C'MON!

CLUNK! GRIND! THUD!

164

THAT CAP WAS HANDMADE BY AN 80-YEAR-OLD HATTER I MET AT AN I.R.A. MARCH IN BELFAST!

ADDLE-BRAINED **COW!**

RRRR

RRRR

BELFAST? MAGEE, YOU ARE **SO** FULL OF...

EOGHAN O'HANNAGAIN!

ZOOOOM!

JUST GOT **AN EMAIL** FROM HIM LAST WEEK...OFFERED ME **AN APPRENTICESHIP** AT HIS HATTERY!

OH BROTHER...

WELL, **BEFORE HATS,** YOU HAVE TO MASTER... **HEAVY TRASH DAY!**

RRRRR

WE **BUY** STUFF, IT WEARS OUT OR BREAKS, WE TOSS IT OUT AND BUY **NEW STUFF.**

TAKE EVERY-THING YOU CAN **LIFT.**

HEH HEH HEH. CHECK **THIS** OUT!

LOOKS LIKE AN **ENRAGED SPORTS FAN** PUNCHED THE TV!

...OR SOMEONE UPSET WITH THE SCORE ON **"DANCING WITH THE STARS"**!

MANUFACTURERS DON'T WANT GOODS TO LAST A LONG TIME. **THE AVERAGE LIFE SPAN** OF A REFRIGERATOR IS JUST 13 YEARS. A WASHING MACHINE IS 10 YEARS. A MICROWAVE OVEN IS 9 YEARS. IT'S CALLED **BUILT-IN OBSOLESCENCE.**

AND NOW OUR BELOVED **GADGETS** HAVE BECOME A HUGE DISPOSAL PROBLEM. THERE ARE WELL OVER **300 MILLION** P.C.S IN USE IN THE U.S. AND OVER **1.6 BILLION** WORLDWIDE! THE E.P.A. ESTIMATES THAT THERE ARE ALMOST **THREE TIMES** THAT NUMBER THAT ARE OBSOLETE AND MOTHBALLED.

LEAVE THE **ELECTRONICS** FOR WOODY. MOST OF THAT STUFF HAS **NASTY BITS** THAT CAN'T GO INTO A LANDFILL.

AND TAKE ONLY **SMALL** FURNITURE.

THE **BIG STUFF** WILL FILL UP BETTY **TOO FAST.** WE'LL BE MAKING **EXTRA TRIPS** TO THE DUMP ON THIS CURSED DAY AS IT IS.

CLUNK!

BUILT-IN OBSOLESCENCE KEEPS THE ECONOMY **HUMMING.** MANY ECONOMISTS ARGUE IT'S A **VITAL COMPONENT** OF THE SYSTEM. **WE** NEVER STOP REPLACING STUFF, **STORES** NEVER STOP SELLING STUFF, AND **FACTORIES** NEVER STOP MAKING STUFF.

RRRRR

THE DOWNSIDE, OF COURSE, IS WE ALSO NEVER STOP **THROWING STUFF AWAY.**

CLOMP!

WHAT'S **THE REPORT?**

N-N-NOTHING UNEXPECTED.

YOU'RE LEAVING **TOO MUCH** FOR CYCLOPS. TAKE **EVERYTHING** YOU CAN. **GOT IT?**

VILL
SERV

OK, BUT BETTY WILL **FILL UP** FASTER.

DID I **ASK** FOR AN ARGUMENT?

WHERE'S MAGEE?

RIGHT HERE!!

GAAAAAA! DON'T SNEAK UP ON ME LIKE THAT!

HEH HEH HEH. GET **THAT!** WILE E. DOESN'T LIKE PEOPLE SNEAKING UP ON **HIM!**

YOU NEARLY GAVE ME **A CARDIAC,** YOU DEFECATING LUNATIC!

YOU SHOULD **CLEAN THAT UP,** MAGEE.

IT'S WHAT THE BOURGEOIS LITTLE TWERPS **DESERVE!**

I **REFUSE** TO PARTICIPATE IN THIS DISCUSSION.

OH GOOD. HERE COMES THE **FREEZING RAIN.**

WHAT TH' HECK...?

RRRRRR

AN **OLD WOODEN PHONE BOOTH!** WHERE DO PEOPLE **GET** STUFF LIKE THIS?

LEAVE IT?

NOPE. WILE E.'S ORDERS.

IT'S FOR YOU. IT'S **YOUR LIFE** CALLING. IT WANTS TO KNOW "WHAT THE HELL?"

GRUNT!

CRASH!

ANOTHER NIGHT AT THE PUB. I **GUESS** IT BEATS STAYING HOME AND DROOLING AT ESPN LIKE **MOST** IN THIS TOWN.

THE **SUBURBAN ENNUI** OF BRAIN-DEAD VILLAGERS.

USED TO BE I'D DRIVE INTO THE CITY FOR FUN. NOW I'M **TOO BEAT** AFTER WORK.

SAPPED OF THE WILL TO LIVE AT **22!**

THAT'S WHY **I** PRACTICE **SVAROOPA YOGA.** IT ACCENTUATES THE DEVELOPMENT OF A **TRANSCENDENT INNER EXPERIENCE...**

...AND KEEPS **MY** PARTY BATTERIES **FULLY CHARGED!**

HARD TO BELIEVE **MAGEESIAN PHILOSOPHY** HASN'T CAUGHT ON WITH THE MASSES.

HEY, GUYS.

HI, LIZ.

MAGEE, **NO DRAMATICS** TONIGHT, OK?

HEH.

WHATCHUWANT, J.B.?

I'LL HAVE A LARGE SAUSAGE, A BAG OF CHARLES CHIPS, AND AN ELIOT NESS LAGER.

AND **I'LL** HAVE...

SMALL CHEESE PIZZA, GLASS OF WATER.

HEH. HEH.

ONE OF THESE DAYS, YOU'LL SPEND **MORE** THAN $5 ON A MEAL HERE, MAGEE.

HOW'S **BIZ** AT THE GRAVEYARD? WHAT **IS IT** YOU DO WHEN THE GROUND IS **FROZEN LIKE ROCK?**

PEOPLE **STILL** CROAK AND WE GOTTA **PLANT 'EM.** BACKHOE CUTS THROUGH IT.

THEY ONLY CALL IT CLASS WAR WHEN

NOT THAT DUMBASS VILLAGERS GIVE US **ANY** SLACK!

Singin' Dog RECORDS

SOME **AGED HARRIDAN** WENT **BATSHIT** MONDAY WHEN I TOLD HER WE CAN'T SET HER HUBBY'S STONE UNTIL **MAY!**

THEY ONLY CALL IT CLASS WAR WHEN WE FIGHT ACL

THANKS, LIZ.

I PUT **AN OLIVE** IN YOUR WATER AS A GARNISH, MAGEE. YOU GOTTA LEARN TO **SPLURGE** A LITTLE.

HEH. HEH. HEH.

BEER

GEEZ, MAN, CUT THE WIDOW LADY **A BREAK!** HER HUSBAND DIED.

GRIEF IS **NO EXCUSE** FOR IGNORANCE... **OR** FOR ANNOYING ME.

DANG! AND I THOUGHT **I** WAS HARD ON THE VILLAGERS!

THEY ONLY CALL IT CLASS WAR WHEN WE FIGHT BACK

174

MAKE THAT ORDER **TO GO**, WILLYA, LIZ?

ALL RIGHT, CHUMP, HOW DO Y...

POW‼

YOU NEED **HELP** WITH MAGEE?

NAH, THANKS.

LOOKS LIKE IT'S **ALREADY OVER** ANYWAY...

YEA!

DUDE!

I GOT YOUR **FOOD**, AND YOUR **COAT**, MAGEE, SO YOU **DON'T** HAVE TO GO BACK IN.

C'MON **HOME** WHEN YOU'RE READY.

CRAZY.

WHEN WILL HE LEARN?

YOU KIDDING? HE'S GETTING IN **MORE** BRAWLS, **NOT** LESS!

HE READS TOO MUCH **BRENDAN BEHAN** AND **NORMAN MAILER**, GETS INSPIRED...AND THEN GETS **FLATTENED!**

WHO WAS HE MIXING IT UP WITH **THIS** TIME?

DARREN TATE! REMEMBER **THAT** PSYCHO?

TATE!?! THAT GUY HAS **DONE TIME!**

YEAH, I THINK YOU'RE **RIGHT** ABOUT THAT. SOME **DRUG BUST.**

HE'S A REAL DIM-WITTED **BRUTE.**

STILL...YOU **GOTTA** ADMIRE MAGEE'S **FIGHTING SPIRIT**...

...JUST **NOT** HIS **FIGHTING SKILL.**

VILLAGE PUB

PIZZA SPECIAL TONIGHT

UUUUUUH.

SO NICE OF YOU TO STOP BY, MIKE.

MY MOM SENT SOME STEW.

OH, BLESS HER. DAD IS IN TH' FAMILY ROOM...

HI, MARV! JUST WANTED TO SEE HOW YOU WERE.

THEY WON'T LET ME SMOKE!

KOFF.

NO CIGARETTES, TH' DOCTOR SAID. AND MY DAUGHTER WON'T LEMME HAVE FRIED CHICKEN. I ALWAYS GIT CHICKEN FROM TH' DINER ON SATURDAY.

WELL, THE E.M.T.S DID FIND YOU ON YOUR KITCHEN FLOOR. YOU'D BEEN THERE A COUPLE DAYS!

SUMBITCH VILLAGE PENCIL PUSHERS BOOTED ME OUTTA MY JOB! FIFTY-THREE YEARS I WUZ DOGCATCHER. GRUMBLE. MUTTER.

KOFF. KOFF.

AW, YOU'LL BE ON YOUR FEET SOON, MARV.

THIS AIN'T LIVIN'. I'LL BE DEAD IN A MONTH.

KOFF. THEM SUMBITCH DOGS ARE STILL OUT THERE, TOO.

KOFF!

UGH. **THE HEIGHTS.** WHERE ALL THE HILLBILLIES LIVE.

THE HOUSES ARE **CLOSER TOGETHER** HERE. SO IT TAKES **FOREVER.**

HOW'S MAGEE?

DISAPPEARED! HAVEN'T SEEN HIM SINCE THE FIGHT.

HE'LL **RESURFACE** WITH SOME RIDICULOUS TALE. HE WAS PLAYING WITH A **HONKY-TONK BAND...**

...OR WAS HELPING A FRIEND **REBUILD A TRANSMISSION** ON A '59 DESOTO.

YEAH, BUT HE MAY ACTUALLY HAVE **DONE** THOSE THINGS!

TRUE. WITH MAGEE, DELUSION AND REALITY **OFTEN** OVERLAP.

GROAN. **NO END** IN SIGHT.

WHO GENERATES THE MOST TRASH? **THE POOR,** RIGHT? MAKES SENSE. THEY'RE LESS EDUCATED, AND LESS SOPHISTICATED, AND THEIR YARDS ARE FULL OF JUNK...

IN REALITY, IT'S THE **EXACT OPPOSITE!** THE **HIGHER** THE INCOME BRACKET, THE MORE TRASH SOMEONE GENERATES.

RRRRRRR

YAAA!

BLORT!!

SCHLU UUUP!

ARE YOU INSANE!?!

HEH HEH HEH! DON'T BE SUCH A BABY.

FINALLY! THAT'S THE LAST OF 'EM.

SPLAT!

AND HEY...THE RAIN IS LETTING UP AT LAST!

NOW COMES THE BEST PART!

SINCE NEW YORK HAS STRICT **POOP LAWS**, MOST OF THOSE BAG BAGS WIND UP IN CITY TRASH CANS. THAT'S MORE THAN **400 MILLION** BAGS OF DOG CRAP A YEAR!

THE HOPPER IS **FULL**. WE GOTTA **CYCLE** IT SO WE DON'T LOSE **LEAKY BAGS OF DOG CRAP** ON THE ROAD.

I'D SCAMPER BACK TO A **SAFE DISTANCE** IF I WERE YOU...

CHUNK!

CYCLE

STOP

RRRRRRRRR

AND THAT'S JUST **ONE** CITY!

MOTHER M-M-MARY!

PLOP.

RRRRRRRRRR

POP!
SQUIRT!
POP! POP! POP!

194

TOSS SOME MORE BAGS ON TOP OF THE POOP SMEAR IN TH' HOPPER.

WE'LL CYCLE AGAIN AND THAT'LL WIPE IT INTO THE HOLD.

UNLESS YOU LIKE THAT SMELL!

SOUNDS LIKE THESE BAGS ARE ALL BEER BOTTLES!

VROOM!

THE DICK CAN'T EVEN BE BOTHERED TO TOSS THEM IN A RECYCLING BIN? OOPS. ON CUE...

KLINK! TINKLE!

...HERE'S SAID DICK NOW!

RRUMBLE!

HEY, HURRY UP, WILLYA? I GOTTA GIT TO WORK.

YER BLOCKIN' ME IN.

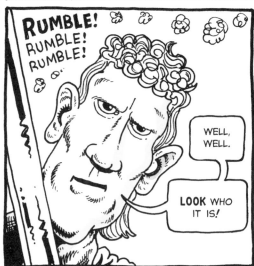

RUMBLE! RUMBLE! RUMBLE!

WELL, WELL.

LOOK WHO IT IS!

YER THAT LOUDMOUTH WHOSE ASS I KICKED AT TH' PUB A COUPLE MONTHS AGO!

RUUUUMBLE!?

HA! YER A GARBAGEMAN? WOTTA TOTAL LOSER!

TINK? TINK?

BRRRAAAAA!

HAW HAW HAW!

SIGH! **DRY CLOTHES!** THIS IS ONE OF LIFE'S **SIMPLE PLEASURES!**

GIMME YOUR **WET GEAR.** I'LL TOSS IT IN THE **SHOP DRYER.**

I **FORGOT** AN **EXTRA OUTFIT.**

YOU **IDIOT.**

WELL, LOOK, JUST **STRIP** TO YOUR UNDIES AND I'LL GET EM AS **DRY** AS I CAN DURING LUNCH.

OK.

OOO...GOT A FRESH LOAD OF **OLD PORN MAGS,** EH?

I'M **EATING** HERE! COVER UP THAT **SOGGY PACKAGE** BEFORE YOU GET HORNY!

WITH **WHAT?**

THE **ONLY** PIECE OF EXTRA CLOTHING HERE IS THIS **BUG-SPRAYING HAT.**

TH' **COFFEE** IS IN HERE, MAYOR. I JUST MADE A **FRESH POT...**

GULP.

GASP!

INFO

BANK OWNED
**PUBLIC
AUCTION**
BIDDING ENDS 5|1

DON'T YOU SEE **THE SIGN**?

IT'S ANOTHER **FORECLOSURE PILE.**

THE OWNERS ARE **LONG GONE.** USUALLY, THE BANK JUST LEAVES **THE LEFT-BEHIND POSSESSIONS** IN THE HOUSE TO ROT UNTIL THE AUCTION...

...THEN A MINION **DUMPS IT** ON **THE CURB** FOR US.

THE BANK IS SUPPOSED TO GET IT HAULED AWAY, BUT THEY'LL JUST IGNORE **THIS CITATION.**

AND THEN HIDE BEHIND THEIR BATTALION OF **LAWYERS.** SO **WE** WIND UP DOING THE BANK'S WORK...**FOR FREE!** NICE, HUH?

IF THEY EVER BUILD **A MONUMENT** TO THE VICTIMS OF WALL STREET, IT SHOULD BE A GIANT STATUE OF A **FORECLOSURE PILE!**

OH GEEZ...

ShoeBarn

IT'S A SHOE BOX FULL OF **FAMILY PHOTOS.**

SIZE 6

204

"WE TRUCK TH' TRASH OUT TO TH' NEW **REGIONAL LANDFILL** IN KNOX COUNTY. OUR **FLEET OF TRUCKS** HAULS TRASH OUT THERE CONTINUOUSLY ALL DAY LONG. TH' DRIVING PUBLIC HAS NO IDEA TH' HIGHWAY IS **FULL** OF ROLLING GARBAGE!"

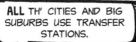

KNOX COUNTY? THERE'S NOTHING OUT THERE BUT **AMISH FARMS** AND **CRAZY MILITIA TYPES!**

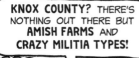

AND THEM HUGE **FACTORY FARMS.** PUT A DUMP NEXTA 100,000 PIGS AND **FOLKS** WON'T NOTICE... STENCH-WISE, THAT IS.

NO ONE WANTS A DUMP NEAR A TOWN, SO THESE TRANSFER STATIONS ARE TH' **WAY TO GO.**

YER IN AND OUT IN **MINUTES** AND BACK ON YER RUN.

ALL TH' CITIES AND BIG SUBURBS USE TRANSFER STATIONS.

YEAH, OUR BOSS MIGHT PAY TO USE YOUR PLACE ONCE THE LOCAL DUMP **CLOSES.**

I'M A LITTLE **SURPRISED** BY THAT MYSELF.

MOST OF THE **SMALL TOWNS** ARE FARMIN' OUT THEIR TRASH COLLECTION TO **PRIVATE COMPANIES.** AIN'T NO CHEAPER, BUT LESS OF A HEADACHE, I GUESS.

BITE YOUR TONGUE! IF THE VILLAGE DOES **THAT,** WE **LOSE** OUR JOBS!

RRRRRR

IT **DOESN'T** SMELL ALL THAT BAD IN HERE.

TRASH **ISN'T** HERE LONG. IT **DON'T COOK** LIKE IT DOES AT TH' DUMP.

AND BY DAY'S END, IT'S **ALL GONE.**

WE ALSO GOT A POWERFUL **VENTILATION SYSTEM** THAT GOBBLES UP TH' ODORS, SO TH' NEIGHBORS DON'T COMPLAIN.

"A RESIDENTIAL NEIGHBORHOOD BUTTS RIGHT UP AGAINST TH' BACK OF OUR PROPERTY. MOST OF THEM FOLKS **DON'T** EVEN KNOW WE'RE HERE."

OK, YOU ALL HAVE YOUR **ASSIGNMENTS.** OH...ONE MORE THING. WE'RE SENDING **FLOWERS** TO THE FUNERAL HOME FOR **MARV'S SERVICE.** THERE'S **A CARD** IN MY OFFICE IF YOU WANT TO SIGN IT.

I DIDN'T THINK HE'D **EVER** CROAK! WHAT **WAS** HE, 103?

HE WAS 81. HE **TOLD** ME HE'D BE **DEAD** IN **A MONTH.** HE WAS JUST ABOUT RIGHT.

MARV WAS A VILLAGE **INSTITUTION.**

HE WAS A MISERABLE **OLD TURD.** GOOD RIDDANCE.

OK.

COME ON. LET'S ROLL.

HOLD IT, YOU TWO.

UH-OH.

WE'RE STARTING **ROAD-BERM MOWING** NEXT WEEK. YOU NEED TO DO **A SWEEP** BY **THE HIGHWAY EXIT** AND PICK UP ALL THE...

...**YELLOW TORPEDOES!**

GROAN!

RRRRRRR

WE SHOULD SWING BY THE **TRUCK STOP** AFTER WE'RE DONE AND PUT THESE ALL **BACK** IN **THE COOLER.** GIVE TH' TRUCKERS A TASTE OF THEIR "OWN MEDICINE"!

HA!

RUSTLE! RUSTLE!

BINGO.

RUSTLE! RUSTLE!

(THUD!)

HOW MANY TRUCKER BOMBS ARE OUT THERE? NO ONE KNOWS FOR SURE, BUT UTAH CLEANS UP **30,000** OF THEM A YEAR! THAT'S **ONLY** THE ONES THAT GET PICKED UP...AND THAT'S JUST **ONE STATE!** MOST MOWERS ARE NOW FITTED WITH **PLASTIC SHIELDS** SO THE DRIVERS AREN'T DOUSED WITH **EXPLODING URINE BOTTLES.**

BZZZZZ

BOOSH!

NOTHING **SUMS UP** OUR GARBAGE PROBLEM LIKE **YELLOW TORPEDOES.** NOT ONLY IS IT AN UTTERLY **DISGUSTING** THING, BUT BECAUSE DRIVERS MOST OFTEN USE DRINK BOTTLES MADE OF **P.E.T. PLASTIC** AS THEIR PORTABLE URINALS, THE BOTTLES LAY THERE ON THE SIDE OF THE ROAD—LIKELY **MILLIONS** OF THEM!—UNTIL SOMEONE PICKS THEM UP. **P.E.T.** IS MADE FROM OIL AND DOES **NOT** BIODEGRADE. THEY'RE A HUGE DISPOSAL PROBLEM ON THEIR OWN. WE USE **OVER 50 BILLION** P.E.T. WATER BOTTLES A YEAR, AND EVEN THOUGH THEY **CAN** BE RECYCLED, ONLY ABOUT **3 IN 10** ARE.

THE **REST** WIND UP IN LANDFILLS, OR IN DITCHES, OR BOBBING IN THE SURF.

HOW MANY FOR YOU?

THIRTY-SEVEN TORPEDOES! OH, AND TWO **BAGGIES OF PEE.**

WOW. I **ONLY** GOT 31. YOU "WIN"!

NOW I HAVE TO WHIZ!

RRRRRR

211

WOW. THIS PLACE IS A **REAL DUMP.** I REMEMBER WHEN WOODY'S **FOLKS** RAN THIS FARM. MY MOM USED TO BUY **VEGETABLES** HERE. IT WAS A REAL NICE PLACE BACK THEN.

YEAH, WELL, **DOESN'T** LOOK LIKE WOODY HAS GROWN ANY **CROPS** IN A WHILE.

WHOA.

THERE'S LIKE **20** **POT PLANTS** IN HERE!

MY BROTHER **TOLD** ME WOODY WAS **A DEALER.**

WOW. **WONDER** WHAT THESE PLANTS ARE **WORTH?**

WORTH **10 TO 20** IN **THIS** STATE, **THAT'S** WHAT!

CURT

C'MON. LET'S SPLIT.

CURT

RRRRRRR

YO, CURTIS!

DORKS.

WOODY! WHAT HAPPENED?

HE **FINALLY** GOT BUSTED FOR **STEALING VILLAGE SUPPLIES.** COPS FOUND ALL SORTS OF **PILFERED STUFF** STASHED AT HIS FARM. SUE ROBINSON **SACKED HIS ASS** TODAY.

YEARS OVERDUE!

NOT EVEN WILE E. COULD **SAVE HIM.**

WHY DID WILE E. **COVER** FOR THAT CREEP? I KNOW HE WAS **A COUSIN** OR SOMETHING...

YOU GOT IT. THIS TOWN HAS **ALWAYS** BEEN RUN BY **FIVE PIONEER FAMILIES** THAT HAVE **INBRED** FOR THE LAST 150 YEARS...

EVERY **TEN YEARS** OR SO, THERE'S A CHANGE IN **RULING CLANS...**

SO WE GET OUR NEW **BROAD MAYOR** AND SHE HIRES ALL **HER** RELATIVES...

...AND THE **CREEPS AND DUMBASSES** OF THE PREVIOUS REGIME GET **WHACKED...**

...AND ARE **REPLACED** WITH **NEW** CREEPS AND DUMBASSES.

DID **THE COPS** FIND ALL THOSE **POT PLANTS** IN HIS GREENHOUSE?

IS HE FACING LIKE A DOZEN **FELONY DRUG CHARGES?**

NOPE.

BUNCHA STONERS BROKE IN AND **STOLE** HIS CROP A COUPLE DAYS AGO.

SOMEONE MUSTA TIPPED 'EM OFF. WOODY WAS **PISSED.**

BUT I BET **NOW** HE THINKS THAT WAS SOME **STROKE OF LUCK,** HUH?

CHUG.

FEH. I **DON'T** LIKE THIS PLACE AS MUCH AS THE **VILLAGE PUB.**

YEAH, WELL, WE **DON'T** WANT TO RUN INTO DARREN TATE, DO WE? IF HE **EVER** FIGURES OUT **WHO** FILLED HIS MAILBOX WITH **SOGGY DOG CRAP**, IT'D BE **UGLY.**

MY ONLY GRIPE IS THAT THIS JOINT IS **A MILE** FROM OUR APARTMENT, NOT JUST A STROLL ACROSS THE STREET.

THIS BAR SPONSORED MY **LITTLE LEAGUE TEAM,** YA KNOW!

BUNCHA EIGHT-YEAR-OLDS WITH A BOOZE JOINT **EMBLAZONED** ON OUR JERSEYS.

IT WAS **HILARIOUS.**

NO DOUBT A **POWERHOUSE** TEAM!

WE **DIDN'T** WIN A SINGLE GAME.

GONE!?! JUST LIKE **THAT**? WHERE DID HE **GO**?

PRRRRRRR

NO *CLUE!* HIS MOM **WON'T** TELL ME. MAGEE MUST HAVE **SWORN HER TO SILENCE** BEFORE HE FLED INTO EXILE.

HE LEFT BEHIND A **PILE OF UNPAID BILLS.** THE LANDLORD IS THREATENING TO TAKE **ME** TO COURT! AND MAGEE JUST **VANISHED.** HE DIDN'T EVEN **GIVE NOTICE** AT THE CEMETERY. WHO KNOWS WHERE HE IS.

PROBABLY ON RETREAT IN A **BUDDHIST TEMPLE**... OR ON A **FREIGHTER AT SEA**!

I, ON THE OTHER HAND, HAD TO MOVE BACK IN **WITH MY PARENTS!**

HAHAHA! IT'S THE **INEVITABLE FATE** OF OUR GENERATION!

AND MAGEE **SKIPPED OFF** WITH THE LAST FOUR MONTHS' **RENT** I GAVE HIM!

SO I'M **BROKE.**

HA!

FOR LEASE 1000 SQ. FEET

ADA REALTY

SIGH. **SUCH A** BUMMER THE **DRUGSTORE** CLOSED.

YEAH.

IT'S **TOTALLY** DEPRESSING TO SEE IT THIS WAY. IT'S LIKE MY **ENTIRE CHILDHOOD** GOT MOTHBALLED.

THE ANTIQUE STORE WENT UNDER, TOO, I SEE.

NOT A LOT LEFT OF THIS TOWN.

GUESS EVERYONE SHOPS **ONLINE** OR AT **THE BIG-BOXES** NEAR THE CITY. NO USE FOR THESE OLD STORES.

SORTA FEELS LIKE THE **WHOLE TOWN** IS BEING SET OUT AS **TRASH**, STORE BY STORE, HOUSE BY HOUSE...

RRRRRRR

OOO, **DEEP**. A PHILOSOPHICAL GARBAGEMAN.

RRRRRR

I READ THAT SOME ECONOMISTS ARE **TRACKING TRASH** AS AN **ECONOMIC INDICATOR!**

THE **MORE** ON THE CURB, THE **HEALTHIER** THE ECONOMY!

YEAH?

IN **THAT** CASE...

...HAPPY DAYS ARE HERE AGAIN!

AND THAT 389 MILLION TONS IS **ONLY** MUNICIPAL GARBAGE! THERE'S ALSO **INDUSTRIAL GARBAGE.** THE E.P.A. ESTIMATES THE EFFLUVIUM FROM INDUSTRY IS A MIND-BLOWING **7.6 BILLION TONS!** THAT'S LIKELY A HUGE UNDERESTIMATE, TOO, ESPECIALLY SINCE THE E.P.A. ESTIMATE WAS LAST UPDATED **THREE DECADES AGO!**

WE'RE UP TO OUR **NOSTRILS** IN OUR **OWN WASTE.**

WE **RECYCLE** MORE WITH EACH PASSING YEAR, AND THAT'S GREAT, BUT IT **HASN'T** MADE A DENT IN THE SIZE OF THE WASTE STREAM.

THE ONLY WAY TO **SIGNIFICANTLY REDUCE OUR WASTE?**

CHANGE OUR LIFESTYLE. **REVERSE** 60 YEARS OF THROWAWAY CULTURE. CHOOSE **COMMON SENSE** OVER **CONVENIENCE.**

IN OTHER WORDS, IT PROBABLY **AIN'T** HAPPENING.

Pitch In!

THE OTHER **BIG OBSTACLE** TO CHANGE? GARBAGE...IS MONEY. **BIG** MONEY. THE PRIVATE WASTE INDUSTRY IS A **$55 BILLION-A-YEAR OPERATION.** THERE ARE VAST PROFITS TO BE MADE, TENS OF THOUSANDS OF JOBS ARE INVOLVED, AND ENTIRE ANCILLARY INDUSTRIES EXIST...**ALL** BECAUSE WE CAN'T STOP FILLING OUR **CANS AND DUMPSTERS.**

⚠ CAUTION

AMI WASTE

AND WHERE THERE IS **MONEY**, THERE ARE **VESTED INTERESTS**, AS WELL AS OPPORTUNISTIC (OR PAID OFF) POLITICIANS. HARD TO **EFFECT CHANGE** WHEN SO MANY ARE HAPPY TO KEEP GARBAGE COLLECTION AND DISPOSAL **JUST AS IT IS.**

KEEP CLEVELAND CLEAN

AS A CIVIC CONCERN, TRASH IS A **HUGE** FINANCIAL BURDEN ON CITIES AND TOWNS. **NEW YORK CITY**, NO SURPRISE THERE, TOPS THEM ALL. IT SPENDS **$2.2 BILLION A YEAR** ON ITS TRASH OPERATION.

AT LEAST A SWARM OF **FLUTTERING GROCERY BAGS** CHASES OFF ALL THE DAMN **GULLS.**

WEIRD THINGS THAT MAKE GARBAGEMEN HAPPY #527.

ANYONE WHO HAS WALKED AROUND NEW YORK ON **GARBAGE DAY**— OR, GOD FORBID, DURING **A SANITATION STRIKE**—UNDERSTANDS WHY. BUT WHAT ABOUT SMALLER CITIES? **AKRON, OHIO**, A DEAD RUST BELT TOWN WITH A POPULATION A HAIR UNDER 200,000, SPENT **$19.5 MILLION** ON TRASH COLLECTION AND LANDFILL FEES IN 2013...

HIGHLAND

MIDNITE MOVIE ROCKY HORROR

BOTTOM LINE: IT TOOK **SIX DECADES,** FROM THE EISNHOWER ERA ON, TO CREATE **OUR GARBAGE ADDICTION** AND IT WILL LIKELY TAKE JUST AS LONG TO **KICK THE HABIT,** IF WE EVER CAN.

IN THE MEANTIME, LEARN TO LIVE WITH **REFUSE** SURROUNDING YOU ON ALL SIDES. AND TAKE SOLACE IN THE KNOWLEDGE THAT CURRENTLY OUR **NUMBER ONE EXPORT TO CHINA,** AT OVER $10 BILLION A YEAR, IS **SCRAP AND WASTE!**

NYK ATLA

EUROPE, OF COURSE, IS MORE ON TOP OF **ITS** TRASH PROBLEM. WESTERN EUROPE GENERATES **SLIGHTLY LESS TRASH** PER CAPITA THAN THE U.S., BUT WITH LITTLE OPEN LAND FOR LANDFILLS, IS FAR MORE **INGENIOUS** WITH DISPOSAL.

THE SCANDINAVIANS HAVE INVENTED **HIGH-TECH INCINERATORS** THAT BURN SO HOT GARBAGE IS ALMOST COMPLETELY **"GASIFIED,"** WITH NO HARMFUL EMISSIONS AT ALL. THE GAS IS THEN USED TO POWER-CLEAN ENERGY PLANTS.

WE DON'T HAVE TO BE **CLEVER** IN THE U.S. BECAUSE WE HAVE **VAST TRACTS** OF BARREN LAND. WE **BURY** OUR GARBAGE BECAUSE WE **CAN.** IT'S NO COINCIDENCE THAT **ALASKA** IS NUMBER ONE IN LANDFILLS.

SOME **GARBOLOGISTS** (YES, THERE ARE SUCH PEOPLE) THINK WE'D BE BETTER OFF DUMPING **ALL** THE NATION'S TRASH IN **A FEW**—OR MAYBE JUST **ONE!**— **VAST LANDFILL** SOMEWHERE OUT IN THE WASTELAND.

HOW **BIG** WOULD THIS DUMP BE? AT THE END OF ITS FIRST YEAR, IT WOULD BE MORE THAN **400 FEET DEEP** AND COVER MORE THAN **1,000 SQUARE ACRES!**

TO FILL OUR TRASH NEEDS FOR THE NEXT **100 YEARS,** THIS 400-FOOT-DEEP DUMP WOULD GROW TO **250 SQUARE MILES!** THAT'S ROUGHLY HALF THE SIZE OF LOS ANGELES AND FOUR-FIFTHS OF NEW YORK CITY! WE'D HAVE TO **SHIP** ALL OUR GARBAGE THERE, OF COURSE, BUT WE'RE ALREADY DOING THAT. **NEW YORK CITY,** FOR EXAMPLE, SENDS ALMOST ALL OF ITS TRASH TO LANDFILLS IN OTHER STATES.

HAVING TROUBLE VISUALIZING A **400-FOOT-DEEP LANDFILL?** HERE'S A FEW THINGS THAT COULD BE COMPLETELY BURIED IN A DUMP THAT BIG.

AND REMEMBER, WE **ALREADY** HAVE SEVERAL LANDFILLS THAT ARE AT **LEAST** 400 FEET DEEP!

BIG BEN'S CLOCK TOWER 315 FEET TALL

NEW YORK CITY'S FLATIRON BUILDING 285 FEET TALL

CINDERELLA'S CASTLE AT DISNEY WORLD 189 FEET TALL

GOOD MORNING, EVERYONE.

I HAVE AN ANNOUNCEMENT.

I'LL BE TAKING **EARLY RETIREMENT** AT THE END OF AUGUST...

GOT MY 35 YEARS IN. I STARTED HERE WHEN I WAS 17.

I'VE HAD **ENOUGH.** TIME TO TRY **SOMETHING NEW.**

SUE HAS NAMED **DIRK** THE **NEW FOREMAN.**

AWRIGHT! PAR-TAY!

THERE ARE EVEN **MORE CHANGES** IN THE WORKS, SO **PREPARE** FOR THAT.

ALSO...THIS WILL BE MIKE'S **LAST** WEEK.

WHAT?!

HE'S HEADING OFF TO **COLLEGE.** GOOD LUCK!

WHEN WERE YOU GOING TO TELL **ME** ABOUT **THIS?**

WELL... YOU KNOW **NOW!**

AND J.B....SUE ROBINSON WANTS TO SEE **YOU** IN HER OFFICE.

HO! THE AX **FALLS,** DORK!

BLAMMO

RATS!

YOU ASS! WHEN DID YOU DECIDE ON **COLLEGE?**

HEY, I'VE BEEN A GARBAGEMAN **LONG ENOUGH!**

MAN, THIS TRUCK **REALLY** REEKS! **UGH!**

AND WHAT ARE **THOSE THINGS** CRAWLING ALL OVER THE BAGS?

AH, THE **WONDERS** THAT AWAIT YOU!

SO ARE YOU LIKE THE **WORLD'S BIGGEST ECOLOGY NUT,** HAVING BEEN A GARBAGEMAN?

THE **OPPOSITE,** ACTUALLY.

YOU LOSE **YOUR IDEALISM** FAST ON THIS JOB.

GARBAGEMEN **ONLY** HAVE TO CONCERN THEMSELVES WITH **THIS...**

PEOPLE PUT **TRASH** OUT ON THE CURB...WE **PICK IT UP.**

DAY AFTER **DAY,** WEEK AFTER **WEEK,** YEAR AFTER **YEAR.**

...AND IT **NEVER** STOPS COMING!

RRRRRR RRRRRRRRRR R RRRRR

241

NOTES

The main sources for this book are derived from the following:

Personal Experience

As I wrote in the preface, I was a garbageman in 1979 and 1980. That's a long time ago, but surprisingly little has changed in garbage collection since then. The main difference is recycling. We recycled very little back then. In 2014, we recycle almost 30 percent of our trash.

Though fictional, all the episodes in this book are inspired by personal experience.

For you trivia buffs, I started on the truck roughly six months after the events in *My Friend Dahmer*. Jeff butchered the body of his first victim, a teenage hitchhiker he had murdered the previous June. He bagged up the remains and set them out for the trash collectors! It was just a few months before I first climbed on the back of the truck. Creepy, huh? Welcome to my world.

I've supplemented my experience with recent fact-finding visits to landfills, both closed and active; to garbage transfer stations; and to recycling facilities.

I also relied on the following reports on municipal garbage.

The Columbia University Biannual Report on Municipal Waste, 2014

This report, conducted every other year since 2002 by the Earth Engineering Center at Columbia University in New York City, is the go-to source for an accurate view of our municipal waste. Until 2010, this report was done in conjunction with *BioCycle* magazine and was titled *The State of Garbage in America*. There was no 2012 report, and Columbia now creates the report on its own, with the more academically cumbersome title *Generation and Disposition of Municipal Solid Waste in the United States—A National Survey*. Columbia gets its info directly from the states, unlike the E.P.A. in its biannual survey. Columbia's report was my main source for the numbers in this book. Garbologists and the private-waste industry also cite Columbia's findings. Even the E.P.A. uses some of the Columbia numbers in its report.

The E.P.A. Report on Municipal Solid Waste

For its report on municipal solid waste in the United States, *Advancing Sustainable Material Management: Facts and Figures 2013*, the E.P.A. doesn't use hard data like Columbia, but rather a byzantine formula of projections and estimates. Its totals are ridiculously low. For example, its 2013 munici-pal waste total is a jaw-dropping 135 million tons *less* than that of Columbia University's. Why? Probably a mix of the usual bureaucratic dogma and a healthy dose of politics. For example, the E.P.A. last conducted a survey of the nation's landfills in 1995! The agency doesn't even know how many munici-pal landfills are out there in the United States! Thirty years without a detailed look at our massive dumps? Incredible. Obviously, there are political forces that don't want this information documented or publicized.

Still, because the E.P.A. has used the same formulas since 1960, its reports are useful in showing trends, even if its totals are laughably inaccurate. The 2013 report was the most recent one available when this book was written.